AMERICA'S LITTLE ITALYS

AMERICA'S LITTLE ITALYS

RECIPES & TRADITIONS from COAST to COAST

by SHERYLL BELLMAN

SELLERS

PUBLISHING

North Square (Little Italy) Hotel Rome, Boston, Mass.

Photo Credits:
Unless otherwise noted, images in this book are courtesy of the author's collection.

Front cover, *clockwise from top:* Artuso's Bakery (courtesy of Artuso's Pastry); Grotta Azzurra sign (courtesy of Grotta Azzurra); Menu cover fom Consiglio's (courtesy of Consiglio's); Frank Pepe commerical portrait (courtesy of Francis Roselli) p. 13-14; Di Palo's storefront (courtesy of Di Palo's Fine Foods, Inc.)

Back cover jacket, *clockwise from top left:* Italy Coat of Arms (courtesy of www.clkr.com); Vintage postcard, circa 1890; Cantina Italiana sign (courtesy of Cantina Italiana); Lasagna dish (courtesy of Grotta Azzurra); Front building facade of Caffé Vittoria (courtesy of Caffé Vittoria)

This page: Vintage postcard of Boston's North Square (courtesy of The Leighton & Valentine Co., New York City)

Opposite page: Olive harvest, circa 1900 (courtesy of Colavita USA)

Pages 6-7: (courtesy of Il Cortile)

Published by Sellers Publishing, Inc.

Sellers Publishing, Inc.
161 John Roberts Road, South Portland, Maine 04106
For ordering information:
(800) 625-3386 toll free
www.sellerspublishing.com • e-mail: rsp@rsvp.com

Edited by Robin Haywood, Mark Chimsky-Lustig, and Holly Jennings
Production Editor: Charlotte Cromwell

ISBN: 13: 978-1-4162-0609-5
Library of Congress Control Number: 2010923335

Design by George Corsillo/Design Monsters

Note on Recipes: The author maintains no copyright over these recipes and is not responsible for the outcome of any recipe in this book. While somewhat revised to meet a standard format in this book, the recipe ingredients and instructions remain the same as provided by the restaurants. Individual results could vary.

10 9 8 7 6 5 4 3 2 1

Printed and bound in China.

Dedication:

*To Papamar and Papa and to all of the grandfathers and great grandfathers
that had the courage to immigrate to the United States under conditions that
were less than perfect to seek a more secure life for their families.
We are all indebted to them.*

CONTENTS

Dello Chef 3.75

Pomodori Nostrani 3.25

Mista 3.50

Spinaci con Pancetta 3.75

Fagiolini all'Acre 2.75   I Polp-a-Cialled
Insalata 4.25

Frutti di Mare Sott'Aceto 4.00

Calamari Ripieni

La Pizza Nostro Gusto 8.50

7.50

Crocchette di Patate 2.25

Zucchini Fritti 3.00

REGIONAL PASTAS

Spaghetti della Torre di Peppe 5.50

Penne con Rugola 5.50

Spaghetti con Seppie (in Season) 7.00

Noccioline Verdi 6.50

U-Scalciaun 2.50

Orecchiette alla Barese 6.50

Cozze Nere alla Barese 5.50

ANTIPASTI

Tutto: Hot or Cold 3.75

le al Forno 3.75

con Battuto 3.50

Farciti 3.50

VEGETABLES

Cicorie con Fave 2.00

Zucchini alla Parmigiana 3.25

Broccoli Saute 3.00

Spinaci al Burro o All'aglio 2.50

Peperoni alla Casalinga 3.25

Melanzane al Forno 3.25

Zuppa di Baccala 5.50

Mozzarella e Acciughe 3.25

Manicotti alla Siciliana 6.00
(Uno per te ed uno per..)

La Caponata 3.75

CREATED BY DONATO DESERIO
Chef de Cuisine

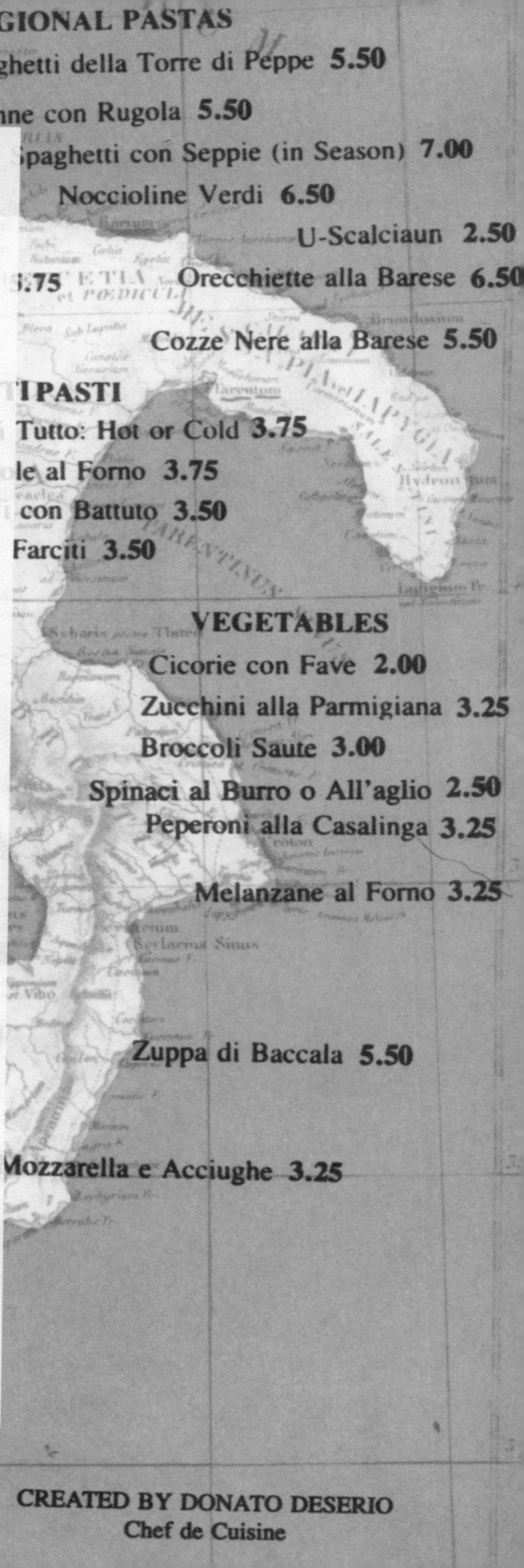

2041— Mulberry St., New York.
The Home of Little Citizens
Souvenir Post Card Co., New York and Berlin.

Postcard of New York City's Mulberry Street, circa 1904 (courtesy of Souvenir Post Card Co., New York)

INTRODUCTION

To Look For America
The Italian Immigrant Experience

From the beginning, immigrant Italians who were just learning English would proudly say that they "were coming for America" – they certainly did that and we are all better for it!

Who could ever imagine a life without opera, pizza, or great art? These wonderful contributions of Italian culture have greatly influenced the American cultural landscape. During the nineteenth century, Italian immigrants came to the United States to forge a better, safer, and more prosperous life. They brought with them rich traditions that included love for romance, literature, science, commerce, style, and of course, most notably — food.

Specifically, it was the Northern Italians who first came to the United States, becoming fruit merchants in New York, farmers in New Jersey, and wine growers and fishermen in California and New Orleans. The greatest number of mostly Southern Italian immigrants (numbering around 5 million) arrived in the United States during "The Great Migration" in the years between 1880 and 1930. At that time, the United States was the largest single recipient of Italian immigrants in the world. They settled here, hoping to find opportunities that had been denied them in their native country, as the climate there — both politically and economically — became increasingly unbearable. As they stepped onto Ellis Island in New York Harbor, the eastern gateway for immigrants, their dreams of a new life were mixed with fears that they would be sent back to their native land. Though this happened to only a small percentage of Italians, the dread of such a fate was so potent that it led the immigrants to call Ellis Island *L'Isola dell Lagrime* or "the island of tears."

This exodus from their homeland of Italy was the largest of any single ethnic group in history, with 1 out of 4 immigrants having Italian roots. These new arrivals were fleeing poverty, overpopulation, and natural disasters. The eruption of Mt. Vesuvius and Mt. Etna, the 1908 earthquake, and the tidal wave that killed 100,000 people in the city of Messina brought massive tragedy to an already impoverished people. The government and the politics of Italy made it nearly impossible for those who were poor and mostly uneducated to make a living there. Working conditions were squalid, wages were low, and taxes were high. Thus, the remnants of crime, which sometimes overshadowed the Old World's contributions, were actually born of the hardships and poverty in Italy. America played a much smaller role in this particular aspect of the culture.

Unfortunately, much of Southern Italy's problems could be attributed to exploitation by its own people. However, the northern part of Italy with its rich manufacturing and more educated population was not completely blameless either. For centuries, the entire peninsula of Italy had been divided into feudal states, which allowed wealthy landowners who inherited certain areas to determine the political and social status of the population. Therefore, the poorer Italians had little chance to improve their lives.

Sharecropping was the predominant way of life for most of Italy's poor, and because they had to give a disproportionate amount of their crop's yield to the landowner, and were forced to pay high taxes, they rarely had the means or opportunity to change their own status.

Some Italians courageously immigrated to America to earn a better living with the goal of returning to their native Italy. Those "birds of passage" who did return earned the term *ritornati*. In the New Country, these immigrants did not want to work as farmers, as that would imply permanence, so they moved to large cities and took heavy labor jobs, which paid very well, so they could return to their homeland sooner. However, a great majority settled for good in the United States and with a spirit for hard work, they forged new lives for themselves and their families, working as laborers, tenant farmers, gardeners, and fishermen. Others became skilled artisans, masons, stonecutters, carpenters, bakers, barbers, shoemakers, tailors, and miners. Those who were educated sought out professions as lawyers, tradesmen, teachers, accountants, pharmacists, and doctors.

In this class hierarchy, the *padrone* system prevailed: in it, the Italian immigrants came to depend on the *padrone*, or "labor broker," to help them obtain jobs in construction, tunnel building, road and bridge building, and the laying of railroad tracks. For a fee, the *padrone* would guarantee them a steady job. The exploited immigrants soon discovered that in order to hold onto their jobs, where the conditions were often deplorable, they had to pay these padroni a large commission. They often felt as desperate as they had in the Old Country, but at least here there was a way to attain something better. As their language skills improved, they were able to escape from under the thumb of the padrone and to create new lives for themselves. By 1890, 90 percent of the public works employees of New York City, and 99 percent of Chicago's street workers were Italian. These immigrants were proud and determined to be in the United States and anxious to make a difference in the new country where they chose to live. They made strides to enhance the greatness of this wonderful country that had received them so generously and gave them the chance to prosper.

The differences in religious beliefs, language, customs, and traditions, as well as unsanitary living conditions due to overcrowding, led to health problems, particularly a virulent outbreak of tuberculosis. Also, during the early twentieth century, there was an outbreak of another kind: acts of discrimination against immigrants, a type of "white-racism" that spread with toxic force and caused Italian immigrants to take refuge in the safe harbor of their own communities. They despaired that not only were the streets not paved with gold, but that they were the ones who were expected to pave them. Hatemongers said that Italians had come to America to do the work that no one else wanted to do. Though the immigrants were ostracized and ridiculed, their spirits were not dampened.

As the immigrants began to move out of New York City, Italian communities began to flourish throughout the country. San Francisco attracted dockworkers, fisherman, and stevedores; San Diego attracted tuna fishermen; Pennsylvania was important for the mining of ore and coal; and in New England, Ohio, and Indiana, stonemasonry predominated. Italians also labored on the farms and ranches across the United States. Sadly, due to the *padrone* system that was still in place, some Southern Italian immigrants were among the lowest paid workers in the United States. Though many struggled with labor issues by striking for safer working conditions and higher wages, a number of Italians struck out on their own, becoming successful entrepreneurs in such fields as banking, food production, and funeral homes.

That the Little Italy communities have remained and prospered in cities across the United States is a testament to the loyalty and pride that the Italian people have for their heritage. The Old World charm is evident in the bright awnings of Italian restaurants, and the smell of fresh bread, garlic, and marinara sauce wafting from them, as well as the music that seems to come right up from the sidewalks. Come for neighborhood festivals, where you can gorge on Italian sausages, cannoli, zeppole, and calzone, and you will think you are on a street in Naples. Although a few communities are being squeezed by the arrival of other ethnic groups with the same hopes and dreams, many Little Italys are still prospering and some are undergoing a renaissance. There is a sense of pride in these neighborhoods, and a fierce desire to preserve their heritage — through food, festivals, neighborhood churches and clubs, and fraternal organizations, such as the Order Sons of Italy in America (OSIA), that give financial and job assistance to their members. At one point, there were more than 2,000 of these mutual aid societies in New York City. These were also places for social gatherings where culture, language, and food were shared. Family is everything and everything is for the family!

For the newly arrived Italian immigrant, meals were not taken in restaurants as that would have meant that Mama was a terrible cook; rather, the meals that were served at home, at the mother's and grandmother's table, were a triumph of

Postcard, circa 1890. A perfect view of the Statue of Liberty as seen from the ships that brought immigrants to America.

excess. These were not just meals but feasts fit for kings and queens, with an array of dishes including meatballs, lamb, many different types of pastas layered with ricotta and mozzarella cheeses, clams, fish, eggplant parmesan, sweet peppers, spicy sausages, potatoes, and roasted chicken, all flavored with lots and lots of garlic, and then, rounds and rounds of cheesy and sweet fruit-laden desserts. The surroundings might change but the traditions that celebrate a love of food remain with Italian-Americans to this day. I don't think any other ethnic group eats as well! With their rich appreciation for food and their love of family and home, the Italian food ethic cannot be equaled.

Distinctions among regions mattered deeply to the Italian immigrant, therefore each region's local cuisine was most important. Italian cooking as we know it now in the United States did not exist when the immigrant Italian came here in the 1880s. Italian cooking was regional cooking as was evidenced in Piemontese, Bolognese, Neopolitan, Tuscan, and Sicilian neighborhoods.

As the twentieth century progressed, Italian Americans moved into the mainstream of American society. The generation that came to the United States unable to speak the language saw their children speak English, graduate from college, and attain the American Dream. With the rise of Italian American writers, labor leaders, and artists came more political clout. Close to 1 million Italians living in America served in the armed forces in World War II and many more worked for the war effort, more than any other nationality. These immigrants were truly Americans. From Nobel Prize winners to opera stars to politicians to entertainers to sports figures, Italian immigrants really did realize their dreams and they were proud to call America their home. This America, which was discovered by an Italian, Christoforo Colombo, and named for the Italian explorer Amerigo Vespucci, owes much to the Italian immigrant who contributed to this country in so many ways.

Generations of Italian Americans have become ubiquitous in all fields, including art, science, music, entertainment, politics, and education. As they have become an integral part of the fabric of American culture, they've also managed to pay tribute to the unique threads of their distinctive heritage. In New York City, Italian American culture has become a major component of the personality of the city. In cities across the nation — from Baltimore to Cleveland to Chicago to San Francisco — Little Italys continue to thrive, teeming with the rich flavors and culture of the Old World. In *America's Little Italys*, I am happy to take you on a tour of these wonderful neighborhoods and its restaurants, cafés, and markets, which bring us back to a bygone era and honor the Italy that lives forever in our hearts.

Sheryll Bellman
April 2010
New York City

Frank Pepe's commercial portrait, circa 1935, with backdrop of his beloved Amalfi coast (courtesy of Frank Pepe's Pizzeria)

PART I

TIMELINE 6000 B.C.E. – 2010 C.E.

6000 – 5000 B.C.E.

6000 B.C.E. — The olive has long been popular with food lovers, but its use extends beyond the kitchen. For many years it has been a healthful addition to face care products and its scent is lovely as fuel for lamps. The origin of olive oil is a mystery, but there is evidence that olives were cultivated by the early Greeks and Romans. The Romans believe that the olive tree first came to life after Hercules gave a mighty strike to the earth. The Greeks believe the goddess Athena created olive oil.

5000 B.C.E. — Garlic, a part of the lily family, is among the oldest known horticultural crops. Egyptian and Indian cultures referred to garlic 5,000 years ago; there is evidence of its use by the Babylonians 4,500 years ago and it was grown in China more than 4,000 years ago. Garlic is thought to prolong physical strength, cure toothaches, and heal open wounds.

800 – 187 B.C.E.

400 B.C.E. — An Etruscan tomb shows a group of natives making what appears to be pasta.

187 B.C.E. — In Italy, the construction of a road to connect Florence and Bologna causes an enormous growth in population, trade, culture, and commerce. The nearby Panna Springs, with its pure water, will one day become home to Acqua Panna water.

1000 – 1200 A.C.E.

1000 A.C.E. — The term "pizza" is said to derive from a Medieval Latin word meaning "a point," which in turn leads to the Italian word pizzicare, to pinch or pluck. The word appears for the first time in print as a Neapolitan dialect word — pizza or picea.

1200 A.C.E. — Dried pasta is marketed by the maritime republics of Genoa and Pisa.

1200 A.C.E. — The properties of S.Pellegrino® Sparkling Natural Mineral Water are renowned as early as the 12th century.

S.PELLEGRINO®
(courtesy of Nestle Waters®)

1200 A.C.E. — According to legend, Leonardo da Vinci visits the town of San Pellegrino while living in Milan.

16

1300 – 1492

1300 — Marco Polo is thought to have introduced pasta to Italy following his exploration of the Far East. This is a pasta myth, one of many that exists regarding its origin.

1492 — Columbus sails from Spain to a landfall somewhere in the Caribbean and "stumbles" onto present-day America.

Christopher Columbus (courtesy of ushistoryimages.com)

(courtesy of ushistoryimages.com)

1574

1574 — Risotto is created in Milan during the time that their great cathedral is under construction. It is said that the master glassworker on the job, who is known for using saffron to enhance his paint pigments, adds saffron to a pot of rice at a wedding party. The response of the guests is, risus optimus, Latin for "excellent rice." It is later shortened to risotto.

1600 – 1645

1600 — Coffee is introduced to the West by Italian traders. In Italy, Pope Clement VIII is urged by his advisers to consider this favorite drink of the Ottoman Empire as part of the infidel threat. However, he decides to "baptize" it instead, making it an acceptable Christian beverage.

Coffee bean plant

1645 — The first coffeehouse opens in Italy.

 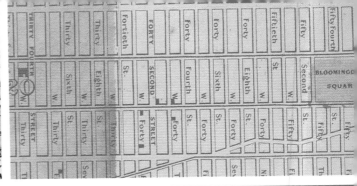

1682

• Italian explorer, Enrico de Tonti, reaches the mouth of the Mississippi River. The town of Tontitown, Arkansas is named after him.

(courtesy of The Tontitown Historical Museum)

1718

• The Amaretti di Saronno® cookie recipe is developed. Legend holds that these crisp, airy cookies are first created to honor a visit from the Cardinal of Milan. Two young lovers bake a mixture of sugar, apricot kernels, and egg whites to create the unusual flavor and wrap the cookies in pairs to symbolize their love.

(courtesy of Lazzaroni USA®)

1770

• Giovanni Basiolo brings gelato to New York City. It is said that he deserves credit for opening the first gelateria ("ice cream shop") in the United States.

(© Kheng Guan Toh/iStockphoto)

18

photo credit: top of page, left to right: map of Roman Empire (courtesy of University of Calgary)

MAP OF
NEW YORK
Surveyed in 1782 and drawn 178.
by
JOHN HILLS.

1781

• Lazzaroni® begins producing its original Amaretti di Saronno® cookies in the distinctive red tin.

(courtesy of Lazzaroni USA®)

1789

• Pasta makes its way to the New World through the English, who discover it while touring Italy. Colonists bring to America the English practice of cooking noodles at least one-half hour, then smothering them with cream sauce and cheese. But it is Thomas Jefferson who is credited with bringing the first "maccaroni" machine to America when he returns home after serving as ambassador to France.

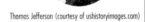

Thomas Jefferson (courtesy of ushistoryimages.com)

• Two Italian abbots describe a "pear-shaped tomato" which has a more delicate and less acidic taste than the round tomato. It's thought to be a possible forerunner of the San Marzano. This tomato may be the result of a spontaneous hybridization of two other varieties of tomatoes.

1840 - 1920

• Between 1840 - 1920, approximately 37 million immigrants, the greatest influx ever, enter the U.S.

19

(courtesy of La Bella San Marzano®)

city of new orleans

1822

- The first espresso machine is made in France.

An early espresso machine (courtesy of Caffé Vittoria)

1835

Our Tradition. Your Inspiration.

(courtesy of Filippo Berio®)

- Filippo Berio moves to Lucca from Genoa to master the fine craft of olive oil production. By 1850 the olive oils are being sold throughout Italy and by 1870, they are being exported worldwide.

1837

- La Louisiane restaurant opens in the French Quarter of New Orleans, Louisiana.

Historic olive groves (courtesy of Colavita USA)

photo credits: top of page, left to right: map of New Orleans (courtesy of New Orleans Italian American Museum); (courtesy of Antoine's Restaurant)

1840

• Antoine Alciatore, an Italian, opens a pension and boarding house that eventually becomes Antoine's Restaurant, the country's oldest family-run business on St. Louis Street in New Orleans, Louisiana, serving elegant French Creole dishes.

Antoines Kitchen, circa 1951 (courtesy of Antoine's Restaurant)

1848

Antoine Zerega, 1814 - 1888 (courtesy of A. Zerega's Sons, Inc.)

• The first industrial pasta factory in America is built in Brooklyn by a Frenchman, Antoine Zerega. It is said that he spread his spaghetti strands on the roof to dry in the sunshine.

1850

• Frances Xavier Cabrini (Mother Cabrini), the patron saint of immigrants, is born in Lodigiano, Italy and will go on to establish hospitals and schools in the United States for Italian immigrants. She dies in 1917 at age 67.

Mother Cabrini (courtesy of N.G.Basevi, © 1946)

21

1860

(courtesy of Gruppo Campari®)

• Gaspare Campari invents the bright red aperitif at the historical Caffé Campari in Milan, Italy. An alcoholic spirit made from the infusion of bitter herbs, aromatic plants, and fruit in alcohol, remains unchanged throughout its history. With its distinctive red color, aroma, and flavor, Campari is used as a base for many cocktails around the world.

• Acqua Panna Natural Spring Water® is bottled as distribution grows.

(courtesy of Nestle Waters®)

22

1861

• The Kingdom of Italy is proclaimed; Sicily and Naples vote to join the Kingdom.

(courtesty of Clkr.com)

1870

(courtesy of Clkr.com)

• Congress enacts the first restrictions on immigration to the U.S. Italians, Russians, and Austro-Hungarians begin to arrive in large numbers.

1876

• Father Joachim Guerrini raises money to purchase the Hooten Estate at the corner of Prince and Hanover Streets in Boston. It becomes Saint Leonard of Port Maurice, the first official Italian church.

1878

• After falling into debt, Father Guerrini moves to New York from Boston to escape his creditors.

• Besieged by increasing numbers of Irish and Southern Italians, the Northern Italians move to other parts of Boston.

1880

• Italy's troubled economy, crop failures, and political climate lead to the start of a mass immigration of nearly five million Italian immigrants entering in the U.S.

23

Ellis Island Administration Building

IN RECOGNITION OF THE CULTURE
ARTISTIC AND ECONOMIC
CONTRIBUTIONS BY ITALO-AMERIC
IN RHODE ISLAND.
THIS GATEWAY INCLUDING THE A
CORINTHIAN CAPITALS AND LaP
SO PREVALENT IN ITALIAN
ARCHITECTURE AND ART. STAN
PROUDLY TO WELCOME
YOUR ENTRANCE.

1885

• Italians and Russian Jews immigrate into East Boston.

(courtesy of Town Square Graphics)

1886

Statue of Liberty

• The Statue of Liberty is placed on Bedloe's Island, the gateway to New York City.

• Fior d'Italia, the oldest continuously owned Italian restaurant, is opened by Angelo Del Monte in what will become the Italian North Beach section of San Francisco, California.

Menu 1886 (courtesy of Fior d'Italia)

1887

• The DeCecco brothers open a flour mill and pasta factory in the small village of Fara San Martino, Italy.

• The Federal Hill House in Providence, Rhode Island is founded to help thousands of immigrants find jobs and homes. It is still in operation today as a social services agency.

Illustration of Providence, Rhode Island (courtesy of Joseph Muratore)

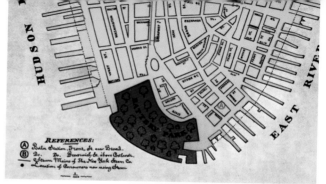

1889

- Hull House, the most well known settlement house in the United States, is co-founded on September 18, 1889 by Jane Addams and Ellen Gates Starr on the Near West Side in Little Italy in Chicago, Illinois. Hull House immediately opens its doors to recently arrived European immigrants.

- Pizza Margherita is invented in Naples by a baker to honor Queen Margherita of Italy. The baker successfully includes the colors of the Italian flag, using tomatoes, basil, and mozzarella cheese, for red, green, and white.

(courtesy of Jupiter Images)

1890

Postcard circa 1890 North Square (Little Italy) Boston, Massachusetts (courtesy of The Leighton & Valentine Co., New York City)

- During this time, the North End and the West End of Boston are the centers for Jewish life. Within twenty years, however, the Jewish community settles in the South End and Roxbury, and the North End becomes the center of Italian life.

1891

- Ronca Brothers Pastry Shop opens at the corner of Broome Street and Mulberry Street in New York City's Little Italy.

1892

• The immigration station opens at Ellis Island on January 1. Before Ellis Island, Castle Garden in The Battery at the southern tip of Manhattan, now Castle Clinton National Monument, was the first stop for immigrants entering the U.S.

1895

ITALY'S FAVOURITE COFFEE

(courtesy of Lavazza USA®)

• Luigi Lavazza begins selling grocery products such as soap, spirits, spices, oil, and coffee in his shop in the town of Torino in Northern Italy.

1896

• P.G. Molinari & Sons® is founded by Pasquale Giuseppe Molinari, a Piemontese immigrant who arrived in San Francisco, California in 1884, at age 14. The traditional Italian art of sausage making is carried on through four generations of family members in the historical North Beach section of San Francisco.

26

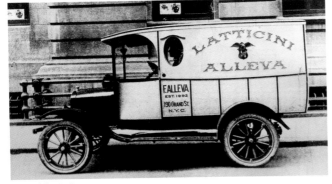

(courtesy of Alleva Dairy)

• Alleva Dairy opens on Grand Street in New York City.

• Ferrara Café opens at 195 Grand Street in New York City.

(courtesy of P.G. Molinaria & Sons®)

photo credits: top of page, left to right: Vintage postcard, circa 1890; Vintage sheet music, 1896 (courtesy of McCarthy & Fisher Music Pub, Inc.); Danny Di Bruno, circa 1930 (courtesy of Bill Mignucci, Jr.); map of New York and Brooklyn, 1876 (courtesy of Library of Congress)

Grandpa and bakers making the toronne (courtesy of Ferrara®)

1899

• The Sicilian immigrants Joseph, Luca, and Felix Vaccaro and brother-in-law, Salvador D'Antoni, begin importing bananas to New Orleans from La Ceiba, Honduras.

(courtesy of Clkr.com)

• The DiRocco family of Philadelphia open Dante & Luigi's Corona DiFerro, a restaurant combined with a boarding house, to attract incoming Italian immigrants.

1899

(courtesy of Nestle Waters®)

• In 1899, the property that is home to San Pellegrino mineral water — popular since the 12th century — was purchased by Societa Anonima della Terma di San Pellegrino. The spring is located in a town of the same name at the foot of the Dolomite mountains in the Italian Alps.

Francesco Dispigno, circa 1894 (courtesy of Ralph's Italian Restaurant)

1900

• Early 1900s Torani® is used as a new flavor in coffee. When it's added to espresso and steamed milk, a new coffee experience is born at Caffé Trieste in the North Beach section of San Francisco, California.

(courtesy of R. Torani & Company®)

27

• The Dispigno family open Ralph's Italian Restaurant in a rented building at 901 Montrose Street in South Philadelphia and name it after their 10-year-old son Ralph.

1901

• During this decade, the largest number of immigrants arrive in the U.S. (The total for the decade is 8,795,386.)

Postcard circa 1890, immigrants enterting the U.S. in New York City

1902

• Angelo opens at 146 Mulberry Street in New York City.

Menu cover, circa 1950 (courtesy of Angelo)

1904

(courtesy of The Original Vincent's)

• The Original Vincent's opens at 119 Mott Street in New York City.

• The Worlds Fair's Louisiana Purchase Exposition is well represented by Italy and Italian art and sculpture as well as rare collections of marble, furniture, mirrors, glassware, pottery, fabrics, silks, laces, and embroideries.

• Amadeo Peter Giannini establishes the Bank of Italy in his hometown of San Francisco, California. His banks expand throughout California, creating the first statewide branch-banking system in the country.

·LOMBARDI'S in 1905·

1905

• Gennaro Lombardi opens Lombardi's on Spring Street in New York City and is granted the first U.S. license to sell pizza. The cost is a nickel. It begins to catch on and Lombardi's eventually becomes famous as "America's first pizzeria."

• Providence, Rhode Island's Italian population increases to 18,000. They replace the Irish as the largest ethnic group on Federal Hill.

• Mamma Leone's opens in New York City.

• Vincent Taormina and Company is established as an importing company in New Orleans, Louisiana to bring authentic Italian olive oil and tomato products to Italian American families.

1905

• The Order Sons of Italy in America (OSIA) was established in New York City by Dr. Vincenzo Sellaro and five other Italians who immigrated during the Italian move of the 1890s and early 1900s. Their goal was to promote immigration legislation, assist in the assimilation process, support cooperation of trade and diplomatic relations between the US and Italy, and many other initiatives including educational, social, and fraternal events. Today, OSIA is the oldest and most demographically diverse association of American men and women of Italian decent.

(courtesy of Order Sons of Italy in Amercia)

1906

• The Muffuletta, the legendary sandwich consisting of a 10" round roll, spread with olive oil and an olive salad, Genoa salami, Italian ham, and provolone cheese is developed at the Central Grocery in the French Quarter of New Orleans by Salvatore Lupo, an immigrant from Sicily. Many try but cannot duplicate this sandwich anywhere else but in New Orleans.

• At 5:12 a.m. on April 18, the most significant earthquake in U.S. history occurs in San Francisco, California.

29

1908

• Grotta Azzurra opens on 177 Mulberry Street in New York City.

• DeCecco® Products develop their trademark which shows a country girl from Abruzzo carrying a wheat stack.

1909

• Italian men in Providence, Rhode Island outnumber women 60% to 32%. Many men return to Italy to find brides.

1910

• Massachusetts General Court recognizes Columbus Day as an official holiday in response to pressure from North End Italians.

• Savino DiPalo opens a latteria "dairy shop" on Mott Street in New York City.

Savino "Sam" Di Palo (courtesy of Di Palo's Fine Foods)

photo credits: top of page, left to right: A.G. Ventrone circa 1910 Federal Hill Rhode Island (courtesy of Joseph R. Muratore); menu (courtesy of Grotta Azzurra); vintage photo (courtesy of Associated Press); Arthur Avenue, Bronx, New York circa 1930 (courtesy of Egidio Pastry Shop, Inc.)

1911

• The first annual Fisherman's Feast was held in the North End in 1911, when the fishermen from Sicily brought their 16th century traditional feast to the United States.

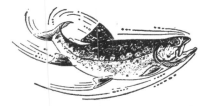

1912

(courtesy of New World Pasta Company™)

• The Prince Macaroni Manufacturing Co. is opened in a storefront on Prince Street in Boston's North End by three immigrants from Villa Rosa, Italy: Michele Cantella, Gaetana LaMarca, and Giuseppe Seminara.

1913

• Joseph Uddo, a cousin of the Taormina family, starts a food-importing business in New Orleans. The Uddo and Taormina companies eventually merge in 1925 to form the Uddo and Taormina Corporation.

EST. 1912

Egidio Pastry Shop Inc.

ITALIAN & FRENCH PASTRY
CAPPUCCINO AND ESPRESSO
WEDDING & BIRTHDAY CAKES
(718) 295-6077
FAX: (718) 295-1468

CARMELA LUCCIOLA

622 EAST 187TH ST.
BRONX, N.Y. 10458

(courtesy of Carmela Lucciola)

• Egidio's Pastry owner, Pasquale Egidio, opens his shop in the Arthur Avenue section of the Bronx, New York.

31

1914

• World War I interrupts mass immigration to the United States.

• A spike in food prices leads to the Macaroni Riots in Providence's Federal Hill. After two days, the prices are rolled back.

32

(courtesy of New World Pasta Company™)

photo credits: top of page, left to right: 1915 banquet in celebration of Rome's new mayor (courtesy of Fior d'Italia); Scialo Brothers (courtesy of Lois Ellis and Carol Gaeta); Di Camillo Bakery delivery trucks, circa 1934 (courtesy of Michael Di Camillo)

1915

• Austrian immigrants Jacob and Morris Teitel open a food shop on Arthur Avenue in the Bronx. In this Italian community, the Teitel brothers are the only Jewish shop owners.

(courtesy of Teitel Bros.)

• Francesco Dispigno purchases a former boarding house and moves his restaurant, Ralph's, to this new location on South 9th Street in the Italian Market of Philadelphia, Pennsylvania.

• Emanuel Ronzoni starts in the macaroni trade in New York, after immigrating in 1881, and begins the company that still bears his name, the Ronzoni Macaroni Company.

1916

• Luigi Scialo, his sister Maria, and brother Gaetano open Scialo Brothers Bakery on Atwells Avenue in the Federal Hill district of Providence, Rhode Island.

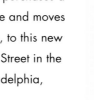

RALPH'S
Italian Restaurant
"Oldest Family-Owned Restaurant in America"

760 S. 9th Street • Philadelphia, PA 19147
(215) 627-6011 • Fax (215) 627-6527
E-mail: RalphsRest@aol.com
www.ralphsrestaurant.com

(courtesy of Ralph's Italian Restaurant)

1918

• Madonia Brothers Bakery opens on Arthur Avenue in the Bronx.

(courtesy of The Arthur Avenue Association)

• Guarino's Restaurant opens on Mayfield Road in Cleveland, Ohio's Little Italy, eventually becoming the oldest restaurant in the Murray Hill section of Cleveland.

1919

• Panettone® becomes widely known thanks to a young Milanese baker, Angelo Motta, who gives his name to what will be one of Italy's best-known brands, revolutionizing this bread by giving it its domed shape.

• Gregorio Garofalo opens Puglia at 189 Hester Street in New York City.

• Giuseppe Migliucci purchases a small 20 x 50-foot store on Arthur Avenue in the Bronx and begins making pizzas. His reputation soon grows and he renames his little shop, Vera (Real) Mario's Pizzeria and Restaurant. It becomes a landmark in the Little Italy section of Arthur Avenue.

• A.G.Ferrari Foods opens their first artisanal food shop in the US in San Jose, California.

(courtesy of A.G. Ferrari Foods)

1920

• Thomas DiCamillo begins his baking empire in Niagara Falls, New York. He bakes his famous panis angelicus ("bread of the angels") for the large immigrant population that has settled there.

Thomas DiCamillo (courtesy of Michael DiCamillo)

33

• Two Italian immigrants, Nicola Sacco and Bartolomeo Vanzetti are found guilty of the robbery and murder of a shoe manufacturing company paymaster and his guard. This is believed to be a crime based on prejudice towards Italian immigrants.

• The North End of Boston is 90% Italian.

1921

- Joseph Campana, "The Father of Credit Unions," opens the first credit union in the country. He starts with $14.25 and after only two years he has 243 clients and over $5,000.

- The debut of the *Italian News*, the first Italian newspaper to be printed in English in Boston's North End.

1924

- The quota system is changed, based on the way U.S. officials view various nationalities. Immigrants from northern and western Europe are considered much more desirable than those of Southern and Eastern Europe Countries like Great Britain, Germany, and Ireland are given generous quotas, while nations such as Russia and Italy are not.

- Joseph Maselli Sr. is born in Newark, New Jersey, and eventually becomes a leader and entrepreneur in New Orleans, Louisiana, known for preserving Italian culture and heritage.

1925

- Joe and Rocco Dilillo, brothers from Calabrese, open their pastry shop, De Lillo Pastry, on 187th Street in the Arthur Avenue section of the Bronx, New York.

De Lillo PASTRY SHOP

ALL OCCASION CAKES • MINIATURE PASTRIES
COOKIE TRAYS • CATERING
WE SHIP COOKIES WITHIN THE UNITED STATES
606 EAST 187TH ST. • BRONX, N.Y. 10458
"LITTLE OF THE BRONX"

(courtesy of DeLillo Pastry shop)

- Concetta Di Palo's opens on 206 Grand Street in New York City.

- Frank Pepe opens his renowned pizzeria on Wooster Street in New Haven, Connecticut.

Frank Pepe's storefront (courtesy of Francis Roselli)

1926

(courtesy of Chef Boyardee®)

• Hector Boiardi opens Il Giordino d'Italia in Cleveland, Ohio. His pastas and sauces become extremely popular. Boiardi changes the spelling of his name for purposes of pronunciation and founds the Chef Boyardee Food Product line.

1927

• The Progresso Italian Food Company is born. The Uddo and Taormina families open another importing business in New York City that soon merges with the New Orleans Company. The company seal depicts a vision of progress, hence the name, Progresso.

(courtesy of The General Mills Archives)

• In 1927, the first espresso machine was installed in the United States. It can still be seen today at Caffe Reggio in New York City.

(courtesy of www.ristrettoroasters.com)

1929

(courtesy of Caffé Vittoria)

• Caffé Vittoria opens on Hanover Street in Boston's North End.

1930

• The Italian population in Providence, Rhode Island, peaks at 50,000, 20% of the city's residents.

• A.P. Giannini combines the Bank of Italy with the Bank of America (which he established in 1927) and establishes the Bank of America Trust and Savings.

• Coffee milk, a Rhode Island tradition might have been brought over to America by Italian immigrants. Milk is mixed with sweet coffee syrup and then heavily sweetened.

1931

• Cantina Italiana opens for business on Hanover Street in Boston's historic North End.

(courtesy of Cantina Italiana)

• Lavazza® purchases delivery vans and contacts customers directly to sell his coffee.

LAVAZZA
ITALY'S FAVOURITE COFFEE

(courtesy of Lavazza USA®)

1933

• Upon the repeal of Prohibition, John DiStefano opens The Victor Café; the "Music Lovers Rendezvous" in what was previously the RCA Victor Gramophone shop.

• The Waterfront Bar in San Diego, California, the first bar to open after Prohibition, is owned by the grandson of Ulysses S. Grant and serves the Italian and Portuguese fishermen.

San Diego's Oldest Tavern
FOOD   COCKTAILS
WATERFRONT
IN LITTLE ITALY
2044 KETTNER BLVD. (619) 232-9656
BILLY BONNET

(courtesy of The Waterfront Bar)

• Illycafe® is founded by Francesco Illy, and for three generations leads the coffee industry in technology and innovation.

1935

• Francesco Illy, an inventor and industry leader, invents the first automatic espresso machine that substitutes compressed air for steam. He calls this invention the illetta.

(courtesy of Illy®)

• Lindo Borgatti begins making his famed egg noodles and ravioli from Borgatti's, his store on 187th Street in the Arthur Avenue section of the Bronx.

1936

Spumoni cart (courtesy of L&B Spumoni Gardens)

• After selling spumoni from their horse-drawn cart, the Barbati family opens L & B Spumoni Gardens in Brooklyn, New York.

1937

• Italian immigrant, Charles Ponzi, is deported after earning $15 million largely from North End Italian immigrants with his "Ponzi scheme."

Charles Ponzi seen at his deportation (courtesy of Associated Press 1934)

37

(718) 367-3799

Borgatti's
Ravioli & Egg Noodles

632 East 187th Street
Bronx, NY 10458

Tues. - Sat. 9 am - 6 pm
Sunday 8 am - 1 pm
Closed Mondays

(courtesy of Borgatti's)

1938

• Mary and Dave Venteroni open Venda Ravioli on Federal Hill in Providence, Rhode Island.

(courtesy of Venda Ravioli)

• Sally's Apizza opens on Wooster Street in New Haven, Connecticut.

• Salvatore and Annunziata Consiglio establish The Big Apple (later renamed Consiglio's), a small restaurant on Wooster Street in the Italian section of New Haven, Connecticut.

1939

• During World War II Japanese, Italian, and German aliens are interned at Ellis Island.

• Brothers Joe and Danny Di Bruno open Di Bruno Bros. on South Ninth Street in the Italian Market of Philadelphia, Pennsylvania.

1940

• Mrs. Tresilla Robino opens a restaurant in her home on Howland Street in the Italian section of Wilmington, Delaware. Soon Mrs. Robino's restaurant moves to North Union Street, where it is named Mrs. Robino's Restaurant.

Danny and Joe Di Bruno in Philadelphia's Italian Market (courtesy of Bill Mignucci Jr.)

38

photo credits: top of page, left to right: vintage ad (courtesy of Ferrero USA, Inc.); Tresilla Robino (courtesy of Mrs. Robino's Restaurant); making cookies at Artuso Pastry (courtesy of Connie Artuso); Nitti's delivery van (courtesy of Tony Nitti)

1945

• John O. Pastore, raised on Federal Hill, becomes the first Italian American Democratic governor of Rhode Island.

John O. Pastore (courtesy of Joseph R. Muratore)

1946

(courtesy of Artuso Pastry)

• Vincent Artuso Sr. opens Artuso's Pastry in the Italian section of the Bronx on August 26.

• The modern-day espresso machine is created by Italian Achilles Gaggia.

• Ferdinand and Mafalda DelGrosso purchased Bland's Amusement Park and Restaurant in Tipton, Pennsylvania and began producing their famous commerical pasta sauce.

DelGrosso family (courtesy of Michael DelGrosso)

1948

• Joe Nitti and his son, Tony Nitti open Nitti's Bar-B-Que in the Grand and Ogden district of Chicago's Italian community.

(courtesy of Tony Nitti)

1949

• The story of the modern-day Nutella spread began when Pietro Ferrero invented pasta gianduja (a "paste" of sweetened chocolate and hazelnuts) and began selling it in 1946. By 1948, his company, Ferrero SpA was born and in 1949, his popular creation was made even more so with the introduction of a supercrema gianduja. The product was so well loved that Italian food stores start a service called "The Smearing." Children go to their local food store with a slice of bread for a "smear" of supercrema gianduja.

(courtesy of Ferrero USA, Inc.)

• Progresso® introduces the first canned, ready-to-serve soup to America.

photo credits: top of page, left to right: Concetta Di Palo (courtesy of Lou Di Palo); Filippi's Pizza (courtesy of Danny Moceri); Mike Greco of Mike's Deli in the Bronx(courtesy of David Greco); Caffé Roma circa 1953 (courtesy of Brian Merlis, Brooklynpirs.com); Danny Di Bruno (courtesy of Di Bruno Bros.); Joseph Canzani, circa 1955 in Sabatino's kitchen (courtesy of Lisa Morekas)

1950

Filippi's Pizza Grotto
FINE ITALIAN FOODS - FAMOUS DELI
THE HEART OF LITTLE ITALY SINCE 1950

•Veal •Ravioli •Spaghetti •Lasagna
•Shrimp Filippi •Sandwiches •Orders to go

1747 INDIA STREET SAN DIEGO, CA 92101 - (619) 232-5094

(courtesy of Filippi's Pizza Grotto)

• Filippi's Pizza Grotto opens on India Street in the heart of San Diego's Little Italy. This market, that also sells pizza, eventually becomes a chain of restaurants around San Diego, California.

• John O. Pastore becomes the first Italian American Democratic senator from Rhode Island.

• Residents begin moving away from the Federal Hill section of Providence due to declining commerce. The population continues to decrease by 10% in the next ten years.

1951

• Mike's Deli opens in the Arthur Avenue retail indoor market in the Bronx, New York.

Bust of Christopher Columbus (courtesy of The Arthur Avenue Association)

40

1952

• Caffé Roma in New York City (formally Ronca Brothers Pastry Shop) changes ownership.

ITALIAN COFFEE HOUSE & BAKERY

(courtesy of Caffé Roma)

1953

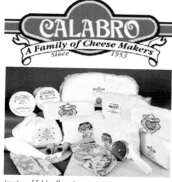

(courtesy of Calabro Cheese)

• Calabro Cheese Corporation is founded in 1953 by Joseph Calabro in Bridgeport, Connecticut. Mr. Calabro was born in Sicily, Italy in 1922. He immigrated to the United States in 1948 after having worked toward a Ph.D. in physics and mathematics and serving in the Italian army.

Mona Lisa
ITALIAN RESTAURANT & DELI

JOHN BRUNETTO   (619) 234-4893
OWNER/MANAGER
2061 INDIA STREET, SAN DIEGO, CA 92101

(courtesy of Mona Lisa Italian Restaurant & Deli)

1955

• Two friends, Sabatino Luperini and Joseph Canzani, open a small family restaurant named Sabatino's in the Little Italy section of Baltimore, Maryland.

Sabatino's storefront (courtesy of Lisa Morekas)

• Stefano Brunetto opens the Mona Lisa Market and Restaurant in San Diego and moves his establishment to the heart of the city's Little Italy 18 years later.

41

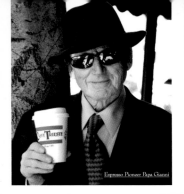

Espresso Pioneer Papa Gianni

1956

• Giovanni Giotta opens Caffé Trieste, the first espresso coffee house on the West Coast in San Francisco's North Beach. Caffé Trieste becomes popular with the Italian community immediately and offers some of the best coffee in San Francisco.

1957

• Rigazzi's opens on Memorial Day in St. Louis, Missouri's The Hill. John Riganti and Louis Aiazzi combine their names to create Rigazzi, famous for the frozen fishbowl of beer.

1960

(courtesy of Consiglio's)

• Urban renewal comes to New Haven, Connecticut, and the restaurant, The Big Apple, is torn down. The owners, Salvatore and Annunziata Consiglio move across the street and name their new eatery, Consiglio's.

• The United States issues a postage stamp in honor of Giuseppe Garibaldi the general who unified Italy.

(courtesy of Caffé Trieste)

photo credits: top of page, left to right: Espresso pioneer Papa Gianni (courtesy of Fabio Giotta); Louis Aiazzi, Martin Columbo, John Riganti with the Budweiser Clydesdales circa 1958 (courtesy of Joan Aiazzi); Rigazzi family photo (courtesy of Joan Aiazzi); Vintage postcard of Lafayette Street, New Haven, CT (courtesy of Frank Rulli); Poster of Little Italy (courtesy of Chris Gomez, San Diego Little Italy Association)

1964

• Supercrema gianduja is renamed Nutella® and begins to be marketed outside Italy.

The *original* creamy, chocolaty hazelnut spread™

(courtesy of Ferrero U.S.A., Inc.)

1968

(courtesy of Solunto Baking Company)

• Mario Cefalu establishes Solunto Baking Company in Little Italy in San Diego, California.

1971

• Tiramisu, a sweet dessert made from mascarpone cheese, zabaglione, espresso-soaked lady fingers, and bittersweet chocolate is said to have been created by Mrs. Alba Campeol in her restaurant, Le Beccherie in Treviso, a town northwest of Venice on Italy's northern Adriatic coast.

1972

(courtesy of Umberto's Clam House)

44

• Umberto's Clam House opens on 129 Mulberry Street in New York City. "Crazy Joe" Gallo is gunned down in Umberto's Clam House on Mulberry Street in New York City.

• Venda Ravioli in Providence, Rhode Island is sold to Alan Costantino and will quadruple in size by 2001.

1973

• The *Italian American Digest*, a quarterly newspaper catering to the Southeastern Italian American community, is founded by Joseph Maselli Sr. in New Orleans, Louisiana.

Joseph Maselli Sr. (courtesy of Italian American Renaissance Foundation)

1975

• Il Cortile opens at 125 Mulberry Street in New York City.

(courtesy of Il Cortile)

• Ella Grasso, born of Italian immigrant parents, becomes the first female governor of the state of Connecticut. She remains in that position until her death from cancer in 1980.

Vintage postcard of Bijou Theatre and Church Street, New Haven, C.T. (courtesy of Frank Rully)

photo credits: top of page, left to right: watercolor of Umberto's Clam House (courtesy of Robert Ianniello, Jr.); Il Cortile menu (courtesy of Il Cortile); making cheese 100 years ago (courtesy of BelGioioso® Cheese Inc.); Grandpa Errico Acricehio (courtesy of BelGioioso® Cheese Inc.)

1977

• The Italian American Boxing Hall of Fame opens in Chicago, Illinois.

1978

• The National Italian American Sports Hall of Fame opens in Chicago, Illinois.

• Colavita USA ® joins with Colavita Olive Oil ® and Colavita Pasta ® and begins to import their products to the United States.

1979

• The American Italian Renaissance Foundation is founded in New Orleans, Louisiana by Joseph Maselli Sr.

• Errico Auricchio opens BelGioioso® Cheese in Denmark, Wisconsin using what he had learned from his great grandfather about the cheese business he owned in Italy.

45

"La Vendimia" olive harvest, circa 1900s (courtesy of Colavita USA®)

(courtesy of BelGioioso® Cheese Inc.)

1981-1983

1981 — Charlie Gitto Jr. takes over the beloved restaurant Angelo in The Hill section of St. Louis's Little Italy and renames it Charlie Gitto's.

(courtesy of Charlie Gitto's)

1983 — First imports of Nutella ® into the U.S. Eventually it is marketed in over 75 countries and outsells all brands of peanut butter worldwide.

1992-1994

(courtesy of Cafe Zucchero)

1992 — The Busalacchi family of San Diego establishes Cafe Zucchero at during the rebirth of San Diego's Little Italy community.

1994 — The film, *Federal Hill,* written and directed by Michael Corrente is released and wins awards in two international film festivals.
The movie follows five individuals coming of age on Federal Hill in Rhode Island.

1995

1995 — After years of neglect in San Diego's Little Italy community, Joe Busalacchi opens Trattoria Fantastica on India Street in the heart of San Diego's Little Italy.

(courtesy of Trattoria Fantastica)

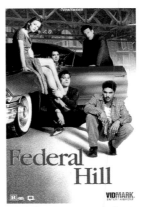

"Federal Hill" movie poster (courtesy of imdb.com)

46

INTRODUCTION

Mangia bene!

. . . America's Little Italys pays tribute to what was most important in the lives of Italian immigrants, and all immigrants for that matter — their love of family and of the food that binds them together.

Sunday sauce, tomatoes and peppers, meats, veal, sausages, and chicken, countless plates of pasta, servings of a wide variety of fish, baskets of cheeses, bushels of fruit, and cannolis, sfogliatelle, and zabaglione, all washed down with homemade wine — these are the stuff of memories from the Italian table. In the Old World, everyone had a garden, everyone grew their own vegetables, and everyone made their own wine. The colorful and picturesque neighborhoods evoke envy for a time not so long ago when food meant family and family was everything. The Italian contribution to the culture of America through their food is unequaled. This book recognizes the vital life of the Little Italys that still survive and prosper today and the people who remember the days when street life was family life and there were no strangers.

In researching this book, not a day would pass when someone didn't remind me of one of their favorite memories from a Little Italy of long ago. Who knows if it was really true that Enrico Caruso sipped a Campari in every Italian restaurant or caffé in the United States or if Frank Sinatra actually had his bread shipped from one coast to the other, but the romance of such lore makes for a good story, and why not? And though such "memories" are captivating, what I also loved hearing were the other, more personal family stories that could disappear if they weren't somehow preserved — the stories of how families that came to this country searching for a better life found solace in their homes with their families and were comforted by the shared foods and traditions they cherished.

The vibrant Little Italys that have survived are a living tribute to the determination and drive of the immigrant Italians who dreamed of a better, more prosperous life in their newfound, chosen country. These neighborhoods were borne of a need for their inhabitants to live among their own, not only because of language barriers but also a need to keep alive the traditions that they held so dear and to shield themselves from the cruel and often critical eye of the outside world.

Many Little Italy communities have dissipated over the years. The residents have left these warm and comfortable enclaves for a more assimilated lifestyle in diverse neighborhoods. The Italian American communities in Minneapolis and Duluth, Minnesota, populated by immigrants from Naples and Calabria, no longer exist. The Little Italy communities in Buffalo, New York; Hartford, Connecticut;

Newark and Hoboken, New Jersey; Cape Fear, North Carolina; Galveston, Texas; Clarksburg, West Virginia; and small towns in Alabama have all but vanished.

Newark, New Jersey no longer can boast of its Bloomfield Avenue teeming with restaurants and cafés where Frankie Valli and Frank Langella were patrons and Fra nk Sinatra ordered his favorite bread to be sent to him wherever he was performing. After urban renewal efforts of the 1950s devastated the community and its dreams, only the memories exist.

The mining communities in Colorado and Montana and the coal-mining town of Scranton, Pennsylvania no longer have the robust Italian presence that thrived there at the end of the nineteenth century. In San Pedro, California, immigrants from the islands of Ischia and Sicily had fished in what was once a large commercial fishing port. Today, the smells of the baccalà and codfish bring tears to the eyes of anyone there who remembers those days, now long gone. Only a handful of fishing boats are left to fish the sardines and not a single cannery remains.

In Pittsburgh, Pennsylvania's Bloomfield neighborhood, in Los Angeles, California, and in the Ozarks (where one of the first immigrant Italian communities in the United States was established), the Italian population has moved on. The once-viable Italian communities in Wisconsin — such as Kenosha, Milwaukee, and Madison (the Greenbush neighborhood) — which were populated by the natives of Palermo who came to build railroads. And Manhattan's East Harlem is another casualty — a once-teeming Italian neighborhood that was torn apart to make way for housing projects.

Places like Seattle; Portland; Jupiter, Florida; Youngstown, Ohio; Long Beach, California; Richmond, Virginia; Frankfort, Buffalo, and Niagara Falls, New York; Memphis, Tennessee; Clinton, Indiana; San Jose, California; Salt Lake City, Utah, Warren and Akron, Ohio; Washington, DC; Astoria, Queens; Williamsburg, Brooklyn; and Hoboken, New Jersey still strive to hold their annual traditional festivals, but most of the residents have left for more diverse neighborhoods. With so much already lost, it's important that the intact Little Italy communities that do exist never lose their flavor, vitality, and lively history.

While there are hundreds, even thousands, of Italian restaurants in the United States serving superior Italian fare, they might not be located in the designated historical Little Italy communities that I write about in this book. As some of the old, established Little Italy restaurants change, trending towards a more healthy style of dining, we begin to understand the differences in the many regional cuisines of Italy and what we ultimately realize is that all Italian cooking is regional. It's not all red sauce! Often, canned tomatoes or tomato paste now gives way to fresher ingredients and most often, Northern and Southern styles are intermingled.

This is a book about the Little Italy communities in the United States, how they came to be, and how they have been able to maintain a sense of community for over 100 years. It is not a treatise on immigrant suffering, or the crime, hardships, discrimination, and labor struggles that they encountered. Instead, *America's Little*

Italys pays tribute to what was most important in the lives of Italian immigrants, and all immigrants for that matter — their love of family and of the food that binds them together. As with all immigrant groups, the Italians who came to America were fearful of the outside world, mostly uneducated, and poor. From the dock workers, coal miners, masons, and railroaders to the men who built the skyscrapers, bridges, and tunnels, there emerged bankers, politicians, vintners, entertainers, and artists. This book is a celebration of the inspiring histories and memories of the men and women — filled with promise and hope and beloved family recipes — who made rich new lives here.

As the first generation to be called Italian American is disappearing, the generation that is replacing them now thinks of themselves as primarily American. Despite the changes in their communities, a fierce sense of pride and tradition endures and family rituals remain the mainstay of their lives. America is forever changed because of them.

That at least fifteen Little Italy communities have survived and prospered is no small feat, given today's climate of assimilation and the increase in neighborhoods with diverse populations. Founded by a once provincial people, these Little Italys have kept their Old World flavor, the richness of their culture, and their immense pride — and we all reap the benefits.

San Gennaro Festival, New City's Little Italy (courtesy of Associated Press)

"To cook like your mother is good.
To cook like your grandmother is even better."
Tuscan proverb

Manhattan's Little Italy

The now vanishing area known as "Little Italy," bordered by Chinatown on the east and the fashionable shops of New York's Soho to the west, was at one time the center of the immigrant experience of dreams and despair. For most of the eighteenth century, long before it was "Little Italy," the area was a 135-acre farm owned by a Dutch family. The farm overlooked "the collect," a sylvan freshwater five-acre lake to the west of what is now Mulberry Street. Unfortunately, industries such as tanneries, slaughterhouses, and breweries began to pollute the water, and the Common Council of New York had the lake filled in. As the topography began to change with restructuring, the "five points" section of the "Bloody Ole Sixth Ward" emerged, and would later make up a large portion of the future Little Italy.

The notorious Five Points neighborhood was the place where the most impoverished immigrants, no matter their nationality, first lived when arriving in America. This intersection was just south of Baxter Street and is where a park, aptly named Columbus Park, now sits after the demolition of the entire block in 1896. This part of Mulberry Street contained Mulberry Bend, the part of the street that bent, mid-block, and was thought to be the roughest block in New York City. Renowned the world over, this was at one time the worst, most dangerous, and most crowded slum in America. Here, there

Chi - li - bil - ly bee____ this is what you see, In I - ta - ly,

The sin-ger sings a song so sweet, the big-a fat-ta Pri-ma Don-na she's a sing-a she no wan-na, there's

mus-ic in the soup you eat, The nice I-tal-ian girl brings wine____ we drink red

Vintage sheet music, 1896 (courtesy of McCarthy & Fisher Music Pub, Inc.)

were constant riots, scams, prostitution, and drunkenness. There were cheap dance halls and theaters, boxing events, and arenas that entertained all manner of gaming — mostly sordid and always illegal.

Beginning around the year 1900, the Italians started moving north from the squalor of the Five Points neighborhood to what was to become Little Italy in New York City. And in 1901, Mulberry Bend was converted to Mulberry Park. By 1903 there were 1,200,000 Italian immigrants living in New York and each year, until 1919, an additional 200,000 immigrants entered the country.

It was in this area of Manhattan that the Italian immigrants settled and created Little Italy (La Piccola Colonia), a vibrant neighborhood that became home to cheese shops, fruit stores, employment agencies, banks, funeral parlors, cafés, theaters, opera houses, gambling houses, and churches, and teemed with pedestrians, dogs, carts, horses and peddlers who sold everything from bread and fruit to cutlery and water.

Bringing with them the spirit of Italian villages known as campanillismo, the Italians would not only cluster together in their communities, they would cluster together on the same block as well. The Northern Italians, many from the Ligurian Coast, lived in Greenwich Village, but the Southern Italians, many from the Adriatic coast, lived in the area known as Little Italy, which included Baxter and Lafayette Streets on the west and Mott, Mulberry, and Elizabeth on the east. The Genoese lived on Baxter Street, the Sicilians on Elizabeth Street, the Puglians on Mott Street, and immigrants from Naples — Napolitanos — on Mulberry Street.

As the Italians prospered, they moved onwards and upwards leaving the area known as Little Italy to the newer immigrants. Initially, many of the Italians worked on the growing city's municipal works projects, digging canals, building bridges, laying

pavement and gas lines, and tunneling out the New York City subway system. By 1890, 90 percent of the laborers in the New York Public Works Department were Italian immigrants. But these were not the only jobs for the immigrant Italian — many found a livelihood in shoemaking, masonry, and operating pushcarts selling everything from fruit to clams. It was the women and children who were the most likely to suffer from the poor working conditions as there were few jobs available to them besides the unsafe and unhealthy sweatshops. Some immigrants relocated to Syracuse, Poughkeepsie, Rochester, Niagara Falls, and Albany in upstate New York to become dairy farmers and others moved to the Bronx to open restaurants and butcher shops.

By 1907, when Italian immigration to the United States soared to its highest peak of around 285,731 per year, there was fierce anti-immigrant sentiment, and the Italians became a target. The United States was in the middle of an economic crisis as a banking scheme to corner the market on stocks in the copper market failed. Knickerbocker Trust, the third largest trust in New York City, collapsed as regional banks withdrew their reserves and the United States Stock Exchange fell to below 50 percent of its value. This "panic of 1907" triggered an economic recession across the country and the immigrants were blamed for taking jobs that should have gone to Americans. Although the crisis abated, the backlash toward immigrants continued until 1924 when Congress passed the National Origins Act, which placed strict restrictions on immigration.

By 1965, the removal of quotas did little to change what had by that time become a trickling of immigrants to the United States. Coupled with a larger intermarriage rate, the Italians had, by the '60s, indeed begun to assimilate into the American way of life. Numerous fraternal, benevolent, and philanthropic organizations offered important support and was the social "glue" that held together the Little Italy community in New

York City. Those who headed these organizations became leaders in the community, working to provide education, resources, and encouragement for the neighborhood. The Church of the Most Precious Blood, built in 1888, was and still is the center of life in New York's Little Italy, offering everything from sermons to plays, concerts, and festivals. The newspaper *Il Progresso Italio-Americano* and publications such as *Il Carroccio*, *La Follia*, and *Piedigrotta* all offered information and help for the newly arrived Italian community.

In the late-nineteenth century there were so many banks on Mulberry Street that it was known as the "Italian Wall Street." These banks served as community centers offering many more services than just facilitating savings and loans. They would double as sources to wire money back to family members in Italy, as telegraph centers, money exchanges, employment agencies, notary public offices, ticket agencies, travel agencies, and wine shops. One bank, the Banca Stabile, dates back to 1882 and today houses the new Italian American Museum in its original historic building, showcasing memorabilia of the immigrant Italian experience through artifacts and photos.

At that time, the term Little Italy did not have the connotations that it holds today. First of all, it was far from little — the dense population consisted of at least 1,100 people per acre. And the neighborhood was not the tourist destination that it is today. Though the smell of red sauce would have permeated the streets of the neighborhood, Little Italy had not yet become known for its clichéd "red sauce restaurants" that now draw tourists. Also, because of the criminal element that was associated with the neighborhood, and the language barrier, the community was not only insular but also off-putting to would-be tourists.

Fish market, circa 1930s (courtesy of The Italian American Museum of New York)

Over the years, the once-vibrant neighborhood was abandoned by many of the immigrant children and grandchildren — of its inhabitants fewer than 100 of the original family members that made up Little Italy still live there. But the heart of the immigrant culture still thrives, as evidenced by the loyal patrons that return each week for their homemade mozzarella, fresh sausages, fresh pastas, and olive oil, patronizing merchants who have remained in the neighborhood and are proud to preserve its heritage.

Today, the Mediterranean way of eating is considered the most healthful and flavorful of all foods. Before the Italians immigrated to the United States, meat and potatoes were the mainstay of the American diet; it was the Italians who introduced vegetables, tomatoes, zucchini, peppers, and the like to the American palate. It is most probably the Italians who taught the world how to eat healthy!

Today the stretch of Mulberry Street between Houston and Canal Streets looks like a stage set of sorts, offering restaurants, coffee houses, and cheese and sausage shops, many of them catering to the tourist trade. A monument to a past long forgotten, this "set" has inspired countless movies, plays, and books. Presidents, politicians, and opera stars never miss an opportunity to visit, either for campaign purposes or to just enjoy a cannoli and sip a cappuccino. And the street life continues each year in September when the Feast of San Gennaro brings families and tourists here to enjoy the sights and smells of fried zeppoli and hot Italian peppers and to revel in the camaraderie that was once the way of life on this famed street.

Il Cortile

125 Mulberry Street, New York City

"A bottle of white, a bottle of red, perhaps a bottle of rosé instead?" Billy Joel's lyrics are said to have come straight from the mouth of an Il Cortile waiter when Mr. Joel was entertaining his then-girlfriend, Christie Brinkley, one evening. This famous song has helped to romanticize Il Cortile (Italian for "the courtyard") for many. But even if you aren't a fan of Billy Joel's music, the romance of Il Cortile, and its elegant back garden room, have the makings of a special evening. Your date may even write a song for you.

Indeed, Il Cortile's romantic, upscale atmosphere and cuisine is what sets it apart. So much so that when the band members of Motley Crü came to dine one night, the waiters were afraid to let them in because of their excessive tattoos!

In what was once an abandoned pillow store, Carmine Esposito opened Il Cortile on Mulberry Street on September 11, 1975. Carmine had lived in the neighborhood, and saw the need for authentic homemade Italian cooking. (By the 1970s the American diner had become a more adventurous eater and the availability of "ethnic" ingredients increased, making it possible to serve more authentic and less Americanized versions of Italian food in restaurants.) As the years passed,

(courtesy of Il Cortile)

Carmine's sons and nephews joined the business and added to the success of the restaurant.

Il Cortile has long been a destination for parties and celebrations among both celebrities and everyday folk. Once considered the "official Soprano's restaurant," stars from the popular TV show used to throw parties here, always making sure that the famous "Sunday sauce" was served, regardless of the day of the week. (The original sauce was made by Carmine's grandmother, who always had a pot of it simmering away on Sundays.) In addition to the *Soprano* stars, celebrities from Robert DeNiro and Andy Warhol to Donald Trump to have dined here.

Everything at Il Cortile is made from scratch using fresh seasonal ingredients. And while the chefs keep true to its Southern Italian red sauce roots, there is always a delicious twist to the dishes at Il Cortile. Next time you go, try their celebratory praline cake that is so good, it is should only be served for special occasions. It is to die for!

Il Cortile's garden room (courtesy of Il Cortile)

Il Cortile Risotto Frutti di Mare

¾ cup extra-virgin olive oil

1 large yellow onion, chopped (about 2 cups)

3 bay leaves

4 shallots, coarsely chopped

6 cloves garlic, coarsely chopped

12 littleneck clams, scrubbed well under water and excess water shaken off

12 large mussels, scrubbed well under water and excess water shaken off

12 ounces calamari, cleaned, bodies cut into rings and tentacles left whole

8 sea scallops

12 jumbo shrimp, peeled and deveined (reserve shells for stock)

3 fresh sage leaves

3 sprigs fresh rosemary

1 teaspoon dried basil

½ teaspoon dried oregano

1 teaspoon salt

¼ teaspoon freshly ground black pepper

¼ teaspoon crushed red pepper

2 cups Shellfish Stock (recipe follows)

2¼ cups (16 ounces) Arborio or other medium-grain Italian rice

2 to 3 cups homemade or store-bought chicken broth, kept hot in small saucepan

In a wide, 8 to 10 quart casserole, heat ¼ cup of the olive oil over medium heat.

Add onion and bay leaves and cook, stirring occasionally, until the onions are golden brown, about 12 minutes.

Meanwhile, heat the remaining ¼ cup of olive oil in a large saucepan. Add the shallots and garlic and cook until lightly browned, about 5 minutes. Add clams, mussels, calamari, scallops, shrimp, sage, rosemary, basil, oregano, salt, and black and red peppers. Add the shellfish stock, bring to a boil, and remove from the heat.

When the onions in the casserole are golden brown, add the rice and stir well. Add 2 cups of the hot chicken broth and cook at a gentle boil, stirring constantly, until the liquid is absorbed, about 5 minutes. Add the seafood and their liquid and continue cooking, stirring constantly until the rice is

al dente, about 10 minutes. If the rice absorbs all the liquid before it becomes al dente, or if you like an extra creamy risotto, stir in the remaining chicken broth in small batches as needed.

Serves 4

Shellfish Stock

6 littleneck clams

6 mussels

1 stalk celery, trimmed and coarsely chopped

1 onion, coarsely chopped

1 carrot, peeled, trimmed and coarsely chopped

2½ cups water

2 bay leaves

1 sprig fresh rosemary

4 fresh sage leaves

10 black peppercorns

shrimp shells

Combine all the ingredients in a saucepan. Bring to a boil, and then reduce the heat to low and simmer, uncovered, for 20 minutes. Strain and reserve the liquid.

Il Cortile's menu with map of Italy (courtesy of Il Cortile)

Sunday Sauce with Meatballs

Meatballs

4 slices firm-textured white bread

8 ounces ground beef

8 ounces ground pork

½ medium onion, finely chopped (about ¾ cup)

2 cloves garlic, finely chopped

2 eggs

2 ounces Pecorino Romano cheese, grated (about ¼ cup)

2 tablespoons chopped fresh parsley

1 teaspoon salt

½ teaspoon freshly ground black pepper

Tomato Sauce

¼ cup extra-virgin olive oil

1 rack spareribs (about 3½ pounds),
  cut between the bones into individual ribs

8 links sweet Italian sausage, preferably with fennel seeds

1 pound pork butt, cut into 4 pieces

1 large onion, diced (about 2 cups)

4 whole shallots

4 whole cloves garlic

3 (28-ounce) cans whole, peeled Italian tomatoes
  (do not drain juice)

20 fresh basil leaves, coarsely chopped

1½ teaspoons salt

1 teaspoon dried basil

½ teaspoon dried oregano

½ teaspoon crushed red pepper

Freshly ground black pepper, to taste

1 pound dried rigatoni

Grated Pecorino Romano cheese, for serving

To make the meatballs: Place 3 slices of the bread in a bowl and pour enough warm water over them to moisten completely. Let stand until softened. Crumble the beef and pork into large mixing bowl. Add the onion and garlic. In a small bowl, beat together the eggs, cheese, parsley, salt and pepper. Add the egg mixture to the bowl with the meat and, working with your hands, knead the mixture lightly until evenly blended. The mixture should be creamy and soft. If not, soak and add the remaining slice of bread. Chill the mixture until firm, about one-half hour.

While meatballs are chilling, start tomato sauce. Place the tomatoes in a bowl and break up into small pieces with a whisk or your hands. Set aside. In a heavy, large (8-quart) pot, heat olive oil over medium heat. Working in batches, without overcrowding the pot, brown the spareribs, sausages, and pork butt well on all sides, removing the meat as it browns. (Add additional small amounts of oil, if necessary during the browning). When all the meat is browned and removed from the pan, add the onion, shallots, and garlic to the pot. Cook, stirring, until the shallots and onion are lightly browned, about 4 minutes. Add tomatoes, half the fresh basil, salt, dried basil, oregano, red and black pepper. Return the meat to the pot. Bring to a boil, reduce the heat to low, and simmer until the sauce is thickened and the ribs are tender, about 2 hours.

While the sauce is simmering, preheat the broiler to high and set the oven rack about 5 inches below the heat source. Using about ⅓ cup of the mixture for each meatball, roll 8 meatballs with your hands, placing them on a broiler pan as you go. Broil until well browned on top, about 4 minutes. Turn them and brown the second side. Add the meatballs to the sauce about an hour into the cooking. Once the meatballs are added to the sauce, stir the sauce gently so you don't break up the meatballs.

Just before serving, cook the rigatoni in large pot of boiling salted water according to package directions. Meanwhile, stir the remaining fresh basil into the sauce. Drain the pasta and return it to the pot it was boiled in. Add enough of the sauce to lightly coat the pasta and transfer it to a large platter. To serve family style, arrange the meats around the edge of the platter and top the pasta with more sauce. Serve the remaining sauce and grated cheese separately.

Serves 6 to 8

(courtesy of Il Cortile)

Umberto's Clam House

178 Mulberry Street, New York City

Everybody knows the story of what happened in the original Umberto's Clam House, just two blocks south of its present location. But, just in case you didn't know . . . The restaurant opened in 1972, and had quickly become a popular spot for diners. On the night of April 7 of that year, Crazy Joey Gallo, an Italian mob boss, was gunned down there while celebrating a family birthday. Crazy Joey was riddled with bullets to his back, lungs, arms, and heart.

Even though Gallo was left to die on the corner of Mulberry and Hester Streets, just outside the restaurant, the waiters cleaned up the place and opened for business as usual the next day. Enough said. Umberto's eventually moved to the corner of Broome and Mulberry where a large picture window overlooks the street in the front of the restaurant — probably, a good idea.

Umberto (Bobby) Ianniello emigrated from Naples in 1934, and began his life in America selling cheeses and wines in upstate New York. His family was in the restaurant and bar business, so

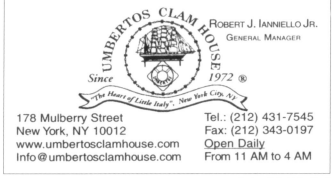

178 Mulberry Street
New York, NY 10012
www.umbertosclamhouse.com
Info@umbertosclamhouse.com

ROBERT J. IANNIELLO JR.
GENERAL MANAGER

Tel.: (212) 431-7545
Fax: (212) 343-0197
Open Daily
From 11 AM to 4 AM

(courtesy of Umberto's Clam House)

it seemed natural for him, at the age of thirty-five, to start his own restaurant. He had noticed that in Little Italy there were few seafood establishments, and thus was born the idea for his restaurant, which he named after the last prince of Italy (as well as himself). Robert Ianniello Jr. is now preparing the fish and we are fortunate for that. Celebrities and sports figures all flock here for the Italian seafood specialties and delicious, traditional home cooking.

Steaks and chops and pastas were added in the late 1990s, as an accommodation to the many patrons requesting a greater variety of selections, but you may want to consider the clams when ordering, if you know what's good for you (know what I mean?).

Umberto's at holiday time (courtesy of Umberto's Clam House)

(courtesy of Umberto's Clam House)

Umberto's Clam House Linguini and White Clam Sauce

24 fresh clams in shell
½ cup extra-virgin olive oil
3 tablespoons chopped garlic
½ cup clam juice (bottled)
2 tablespoons salt
1 pound dried linguini
⅓ cup chopped fresh parsley, for garnish

In a large skillet, heat the oil over medium-high heat. Add the garlic and sauté until golden brown. Add the clams, reduce the heat to low, and simmer for 10 minutes. Add the clam juice and salt. Cover and let steam for 6 to 8 minutes. Toss any clams that did not open.

Cook the linguini in large pot of boiling salted water according to package directions. Drain the pasta and place it on a platter. Pour the clams and their juices on top of the pasta. Sprinkle the parsley over top and serve.

Serves 4

Umberto's Clam House Lobster Fra Diavolo

Two 1½-pound lobsters
1 tablespoon chopped garlic
6 tablespoons extra-virgin olive oil
1 tablespoons red pepper flakes
2 dozen plum tomatoes, blanched, peeled and de-stemmed
16 hard-shelled clams, preferably Long Island littlenecks, well rinsed
16 mussels, preferably Prince Edward Sound, cleaned (see tip)
Salt and black pepper, to taste
1 pound fresh angel hair pasta

Set the lobster on a cutting board facing you (make sure the claws are bound by rubber bands). Insert a chef's knife at the chest line — the point between the head and body where the creases in the lobster's shell intersect. Insert the knife straight downward and then through the center of the head (between the eyes). Continue splitting the lobster in half lengthwise. Using large scissors, cut off the mouth. Remove and discard the olive green bile sac at the base of the lobster head. It will easily fall out during the washing process as it is only slightly attached to the head.

In a large skillet, heat the oil over medium heat. Add the garlic and sauté until golden brown. Add lobsters to the pan, cut-side down, using caution as oil may splatter. Fry the lobsters until the shell is a bright red color, approximately 8 to 10 minutes. Remove the lobsters from the pan and set aside.

Add the pepper flakes to the pan and sauté for 1 minute. Add tomatoes, crushing them with your hands over the pan. Spread the clams and mussels over top of the sauce, cover, and cook until the clams and mussels open, about 10 minutes. Return the lobsters to the pan. Cook an additional 10 minutes over medium heat. (The sauce should be simmering; you may need to raise or lower the heat accordingly). Add salt and pepper.

Cook the angel hair pasta in large pot of boiling salted water according to package directions. Drain the pasta and place in a serving dish. Pour the shellfish and sauce on top of the pasta and serve.

Serves 4

Tip: Cleaning Mussels

Discard any chipped or broken mussels. If you have time, place the mussels in a bowl with cold water for about 20 minutes. This will help the mussels to release silt. Carefully remove the mussels from the bowl, leaving the silt in the bottom of the bowl. Rinse the mussels, debeard them, and rinse again. (To debeard a mussel, pull off the small amount of threadlike vegetative growth along the flat side of the mussel.) Now they are ready to be cooked.

Mayor Ed Koch, circa 1960 at Umberto's (courtesy of Umberto's Clam House)

Little Italy, Manhattan, New York City, Mostoff

Di Palo's Fine Foods

200 Grand Street, New York City

The heart, spirit, and dreams of the Italian immigrant are represented in this sublime food shop that features every Italian delight one could ever imagine. When the market opened in 1914, Di Palo's was a latteria selling just milk and cheese. Today, the shop carries foods from all twenty regions in Italy. With a stunning array of cured meats, 300 imported cheeses, buffalo mozzarella arriving fresh from Campagnia, handmade ravioli, frozen pastas, olives, peppers, regional olive oils from Italy, balsamic vinegars, breads, sauces, coffees, and jams, you won't go hungry. And in the back of the store, it's possible to see mozzarella being made fresh daily.

In 1903, with only fourteen dollars in his pocket, the former dairy farmer and blacksmith, Savino Di Palo, emigrated from his home in the impoverished farming village of Monte Maloni in the region of Basilicata in the southern part of Italy. Settling on Mott Street, already home to many familiar faces from his village and from neighboring Puglia, Savino sold milk that was delivered in horse-drawn carts from Brooklyn and Queens. The system worked well in the colder months but once summer hit, Savino was plagued with curdled, sour milk. A true entrepreneur, he saw an opportunity for expanding his business and soon added cheese made from sour milk. He established himself in a shop on Mott Street and sent for his wife and children to immigrate to America. Every one of their six children were encouraged to enter the dairy business, and, as each married, they started their own latterias in various parts of the New York area.

In 1914, Savino's daughter Concetta married Luigi Santomauro and in 1925 they opened their own shop on the corner of Mott and Grand Streets, not far from her parent's shop. The 400-square-foot store was a true latteria, selling only milk and cheese. In time, and when refrigeration became available, they began to carry hard cheeses and olive oil from Italy. They remained in that location for 77 years.

Concetta Di Palo circa 1949 (courtesy of Di Palo's Fine Foods)

The two sons of Concetta and Luigi Di Palo Santomauro, Savino and Michael, were born in the "fusion" part of New York City's Little Italy, a neighborhood where only Italian and Yiddish were spoken. (At this time, due to social and economic pressures, these two immigrant groups lived and worked side by side.) At home and in the shop, the family continued to speak Italian, but soon it became evident that not knowing English created a barrier, and the barrier prevented the family from expanding their business. Determined to learn English, the brothers enlisted in the military and were proud to have the opportunity of serving in WWII. In the neighborhood, a "wall of honor" paid tribute to the soldiers of Italian descent who fought for the United States in WWII, though recently it was covered over by the new owners of another immigrant-owned grocery store.

Long hours in the shop were not unusual for the family and Di Palo's became a social center;

Ferrara Caffé Ricotta Cheese Cake

1 recipe pie dough for a two-crust pie, divided into 2 portions

3 cups ricotta cheese (about 1½ pounds)

4 eggs, separated

⅓ cup sugar ½ teaspoon almond extract

¼ cup chopped, candied fruit of your choice

Confectioners' sugar, to dust

Preheat the oven to 375°F.

On a lightly floured surface, roll out one of the dough portions, from the center outward, until it is about 10 inches in diameter. Transfer the pie dough to a deep, 9-inch pie pan. Trim the overhanging dough about ½-inch from the rim of the pie pan. Roll out the remaining dough and cut it into ½-inch strips for a lattice top.

Working over a large bowl, force the ricotta through a fine sieve. In another bowl, beat the egg yolks. Add the sugar and the almond extract, and beat until well blended. Mix the egg-yolk mixture into the ricotta. Then add the candied fruit and blend together well. Beat the egg whites until stiff but not dry, and fold them into the ricotta, gently folding over until well blended. Pour the filling into the prepared pie shell. Crisscross the pie dough strips on top of the pie to make a lattice crust. Pinch the rim to flute it.

Bake for 45 minutes, or until set. Turn off the oven, open the door, and let the pie cool in the oven. Dust with confectioner's sugar when cool. Cut into wedges to serve.

Serves 6 to 8

Ferrara Caffé Tiramisu

1 cup strong coffee (warm, not hot)

¼ cup coffee liqueur

1 (7-ounce) box savoiardi or ladyfingers

¼ cup sugar

6 eggs, separated

16 ounces mascarpone cheese or ½ pint heavy cream

1 teaspoon vanilla

Cocoa or chocolate flakes, for garnish

In a small bowl, stir together the coffee and coffee liqueur. Arrange the savoiardi or ladyfingers in a rectangular serving dish (approximately 11 x 13 inches). Drizzle the coffee mixture over the savoiardi to lightly soak.

In a mixing bowl, while gradually adding the sugar, beat the egg yolks until very stiff and the egg yolks appear pale in color, about 5 to 10 minutes. Fold the mascarpone into the beaten egg yolks. If using the heavy cream, add the cream gradually while beating, continuing to beat until very the mixture is stiff.

In a separate bowl, beat the egg whites with a wire whisk or electric beater until very stiff. Gently fold the egg whites into the egg yolk mixture. Add the vanilla to the mixture and fold gently to combine. Cover savoiardi with this cream mixture. Cover with aluminum foil or plastic wrap and refrigerate at least one hour before serving. Sprinkle with cocoa or chocolate flakes just before serving. Tiramisu may be frozen and should be defrosted in the refrigerator for at least 4 hours before serving. If freezing it, do not add the garnish until just before serving.

Serves 12

(courtesy of Ferrara Caffé)

Ferrara Caffé Cannoli

Cannoli Shells

3 cups sifted flour

3 tablespoons melted butter

1 teaspoon sugar

Dash of salt

¾ cup red wine (or less)

1 egg yolk, slightly beaten

Oil, for deep-frying

Cannoli Filling

1 (48-ounce) container ricotta cheese

¾ cup confectioners' sugar

¼ cup Crème de Cacao or other sweet liqueur of your choice

3 teaspoons grated bittersweet chocolate

2 teaspoons finely minced, candied orange peel

½ cup chopped pistachio nuts, for garnish

To make the shells: Mix flour, butter, sugar, and salt together in a large bowl. Gradually add the wine, a quarter cup at a time, you will have a stiff but manageable dough. Knead for about 15 minutes, until the dough is smooth and soft. Add a bit more flour if necessary to prevent sticking. Roll into a ball, cover, and place in the refrigerator for 1 hour.

Divide dough into two portions and return one of the dough portions to the refrigerator (it is easier to handle when chilled). Roll the dough into a paper-thin sheet, ⅛ inch or less, on a lightly floured surface. Cut into 4-inch circles or squares. Place a cannoli tube (see note) from corner to corner, diagonally across the squares. Fold one side over the tube and brush the top of it with some of the beaten egg yolk. Fold the opposite corner up and over the side with beaten egg yolk. Press the edges together to seal.

Heat 3 inches of oil to 385°F. Fry the cannoli, two or three at a time, turning if necessary, until deep, golden brown, about 1 minute. Remove with tongs or a slotted spatula and drain on paper towels. When cool to the touch, remove the tubes, being careful not to break the shells. Cool completely before filling. Fill shells just before serving so that they are crisp. If you do not intend to use them immediately, store them in an airtight container with a paper towel (to absorb moisture) in a cool, dry place. They will keep, unfilled, for several weeks.

To make the filling: Beat the ricotta vigorously for 2 minutes in a large bowl. Add the sugar and liqueur and continue beating for 5 minutes more, or until smooth. Mix in the chocolate and orange peel. Store in the refrigerator until ready to serve.

Use a small spoon or a pastry bag (or a large plastic bag with the corner cut off) to stuff the filling into the shells, filling partway from one end, and then filling from the other end. Dip the end in chopped pistachio nuts. If you do not wish to serve the cannoli immediately, the filling may be kept, tightly covered and refrigerated, for up to 3 days.

Note: Cannoli tubes can be bought at kitchen-supply stores, or you may use clean, unpainted wooden dowels. They should measure 1 inch in diameter and be 6 inches long.

Makes 20 to 24 cannoli

Grandpa and bakers making the torrone, circa 1940 (courtesy of Ferrara Caffé)

The Original Vincent's

119 Mott Street, New York City

(courtesy of The Original Vincent's)

In 1894, Giuseppe Siano emigrated from Italy to the United States as a stowaway. His wife, Carmela, came to America five years later and together they set up shop selling cooked clams, mussels, and scungilli (sliced conch) from a pushcart on the corner of Hester and Mott Streets where Vincent's now stands today. When their son, Vincent, was born in 1904, they decided to move their business inside. Thus, they named their restaurant Vincent's Clam Bar, which later became just Vincent's.

In the same year, Carmela perfected her mother's recipe for her famous sauce, a tomato and pepper-based blend that today comes sweet (no peppers), medium, or hot and is used on everything from chicken to veal to pasta. In the beginning, there was only the hot sauce, but in the 1950s the medium-spicy sauce was introduced, and, in the 1960s, the sweet sauce was added. For fifty years, Vincent's sister, Jay, was the keeper of the secret brew and now another Vincent in the family, Vincent Generoso, (whose grandfather, Jimmy Generoso, was a cousin to Giuseppe Siano,) comes in every morning to make the magic sauce. Today, the restaurant is run by Vincent and it now sells its famous "secret" sauce by the pint, quart, or gallon all over the United States.

Vincent's, famous for its calamari, (Italian for "squid") scungilli, and shrimp, now has its own fishing boat on Long Island to insure that the restaurant has the freshest calamari exactly when they need them! The little clam bar on wheels has come a long way!

(courtesy of The Original Vincent's)

Jay, Red, Murphy and Vinny Boy, circa 1948 (courtesy of The Original Vincent's)

The Original Vincent's Fried Calamari

12 Squid,
All-purpose flour, for dredging
Light olive oil, for deep-frying
Salt and black pepper, to taste

Rinse the calamari under cold running water. Cut the bodies into rings, but leave the tentacles whole. Rinse once more and drain well. Pat the calamari dry with paper towels. Dredge the calamari in the flour, shaking off the excess.

Pour about 3 to 4 inches of oil in a deep-fryer or large saucepan or wok. Heat the oil to 350°F. Fry the calamari until golden brown. Do not overcrowd the pan (fry in batches if necessary). Remove with a slotted spoon and drain on paper towels. Season with salt and pepper. Serve with warmed marinara sauce and a nice crusty loaf of Italian bread.

The Original Vincent's Meatballs

1 pound ground beef
½ pound ground veal
½ pound ground pork
2 cloves garlic, minced
2 eggs
1 cup freshly grated parmesan cheese (about 4 ounces)
1½ tablespoons chopped fresh flat-leaf parsley
Salt and black pepper, to taste
2 cups fresh breadcrumbs
1 cup water
Canola oil, for frying

Combine the beef, veal, and pork in a large bowl. Add the garlic, eggs, cheese, parsley, salt, and pepper. Mix the bread crumbs into the meat mixture. Add the water and mix until thoroughly combined and the meatballs hold together. With wet hands, roll the mixture into meatballs 1½ inches in diameter. In a large skillet, pour enough oil to evenly coat the bottom and place over medium-high heat. Add the meatballs and fry until golden brown. Place the cooked meatballs in heated marinara sauce and serve with spaghetti cooked al dente or use in a hero sandwich.

Angelo of Mulberry Street

146 Mulberry Street, New York City

Angelo of Mulberry Street has been serving elegant Southern Italian cuisine since 1940 in the heart of New York City's Little Italy. In 1902, Angelo Tulimieri, an immigrant from Naples, originally opened a pizzeria named The Red Rooster in the same location where Angelo stands today. In those days, his mistress lived upstairs and worked as the cashier for the pizzeria. They were fortunate to have a coal oven to bake their fresh pizza, which sold for 90 cents, but in 1940, the Silvestri and Aprea families bought the pizza parlor and turned it into a full-service restaurant, coal oven and all.

The restaurant soon became a thriving hot spot for the crème de la crème. Drawn by the delicious food and warm atmosphere, celebrities and dignitaries found a safe haven in this mainstay of Little Italy. Here celebrities were given a secluded area to dine, and their privacy was carefully guarded by the staff. Movie stars such as Sophia Loren, Jacqueline Bisset, Gina Lollobrigida, Warren Beatty, and Farrah Fawcett were said to have dined here. When President Ronald Reagan wanted to eat at Angelo, they created a special menu just for him.

During the 1950s, the Rolling Stones were denied a table because the maître d' didn't think they were dressed properly — they were "not allowed in here looking like that!" The feeling of yesteryear still exists at Angelo, where everything is freshly made to order. Customers feel at home as do the employees, some of whom have

(courtesy of Angelo of Mulberry Street)

worked at Angelo for over forty years.

According to one veteran waiter, Ralph D'Alessio, "It's become my house too." The secret to their continued success is Tina Aprea and her father, who are always in attendance and don't plan to change a thing. There are no computers and they still do everything from memory. The Punchinello, the Neapolitan lucky charm that sparkles in the front of the restaurant has done its job.

Capellini alla Angelo

4 tablespoons extra-virgin olive oil

3 cloves garlic

1 (28-ounce) can crushed tomatoes

Salt and pepper, to taste

Pinch of crushed red pepper

1 pound dried capellini (angel hair) pasta

½ cup grated mozzarella cheese

2 tablespoons grated Parmesan cheese

6 arugula leaves with stems

In a large skillet, heat the oil over medium heat. Add the garlic and sauté until brown. Remove the pan from the heat and add the crushed tomatoes. Season with the salt and pepper and add the red pepper.

Bring a large pot of generously salted water to a boil over high heat. Add the cappellini and cook until al dente, about 4 minutes. Drain the capellini and add it to the sauce. On low heat, add the mozzarella, Parmesan and the arugula. Keep stirring so the cheese melts evenly and doesn't burn. After the mozzarella is melted, divide among 4 plates and serve.

Serves 4

Menu cover, circa 1950 (courtesy of Angelo of Mulberry Street)

Alleva Dairy

146 Mulberry Street, New York City

The oldest latteria in America still stands in the same spot on the corner of Grand and Mulberry Street in the heart of New York City's Little Italy. Not much has changed in this cheese shop since 1892, the year Pina Alleva, an immigrant from Benevento, Italy, opened the market shortly after arriving in America with her thirteen children. She managed to keep the shop viable for many years while living upstairs with her family.

The shop has retained most of the original tiles on the floor and the tin ceiling, which was installed in 1919. The cheese specials are painted on glass signs that harken back to a more charming time.

Pina's son, Henry, and her daughter, Irma, continued the tradition, and during Prohibition the shop, which at that time also served as a café and bar, was closed for a period of time.

Today, Robert Sr. and Robert Jr. are at the counter in this multi-generational, family-run business. It is not a nine-to-five kind of establishment — as everyone who shops here is family in the true immigrant sense of the word — and if someone needs an item, the store stays open.

It was not until the 1970s that meats were on the shelves. Selling mozzarella and ricotta cheeses exclusively did not satisfy the needs of the growing "foodie" revolution. Today, the tantalizing selection of cheeses and meats displayed are as pure, fresh, and aromatic as any shop in Benevento. As they say at Alleva Dairy, made with pure milk, "Sono Fatte con Puro Latte."

FRESH MOZZARELLA MADE DAILY
212-226-7990/7991
1-800-4-ALLEVA

ALLEVA DAIRY

MANUFACTURERS OF
RICOTTA AND MOZZARELLA
SINCE 1892
THE OLDEST ITALIAN CHEESE STORE IN AMERICA

188 Grand Street
New York, NY 10013
www.allevadairy.com

(courtesy of Alleva Dairy)

Alleva's Lasagna

1 pound fresh or 1 pound dried lasagna noodles

16 ounces mozzarella cheese, grated (about 2 cups)

2 (15-ounce) containers ricotta cheese

1 egg

2 quarts homemade or 2½ (24-ounce) jars store-bought marinara sauce

8 ounces Parmigiano-Reggiano cheese, grated (about 2 cups)

Preheat the oven to 325°F. Bring a large pot of generously salted water to a boil over high heat. Add the lasagna noodles and cook until they become al dente, about 3 minutes. Drain the noodles. When well drained, toss them with a little oil and set aside.

In a bowl, add the mozzarella, ricotta, and egg. Mix well and set aside.

Spread the bottom of a large rectangular baking dish, about 13 x 9 inches and 2½-inches deep, with some of the sauce. Then cover the bottom of the baking dish with one layer of lasagna noodles. Dot with spoonfuls of the cheese mixture, sprinkle on some of the grated Parmesan cheese and drizzle on some of the sauce. Repeat with another layer of the lasagna noodles, cheese mixture, grated Parmesan cheese, and sauce until the baking dish is full. Top the last layer with sauce and grated Parmesan cheese. Reserve some of the sauce to serve on the side.

Bake for 45 minutes. Let stand 20 minutes before serving. Serve with the reserved sauce.

Serves 6

Alleva's Chicken Parmesan

1 egg

½ cup seasoned bread crumbs

4 boneless, skinless chicken cutlets (about 1¼ pounds), thinly sliced

½ cup extra-virgin olive oil

2 cups homemade or store-bought marinara sauce

8 slices mozzarella cheese

¼ cup grated Parmesan cheese

Preheat the oven to 375°F. Beat the egg in a shallow bowl. Put the bread crumbs in another shallow bowl. Dip both sides of the chicken cutlets in then egg, and then into the bread crumbs to coat. Set aside.

Heat the oil in a skillet over medium heat. When the oil is hot, fry the chicken until golden brown on each side, about 3 minutes per side. Drain on paper towels.

Pour the marinara sauce into a 9 x 13-inch baking dish. Place the chicken in the dish and top each piece of chicken with the mozzarella slices and grated Parmesan cheese. Bake until cheese is melted, or about 15 minutes.

Serves 4

Alleva's Eggplant Rolatine

1 (15-ounce) container ricotta cheese

1 tablespoon finely chopped fresh parsley

2 medium eggplants, washed, de-stemmed, and peeled

All-purpose flour, for dredging

Extra-virgin olive oil

1 egg, beaten

8 ounces mozzarella cheese, sliced

2 cups homemade or store-bought marinara sauce

For garnish (optional)

Grated Parmesan cheese

Chopped fresh parsley

Preheat the oven to 350°F.

In a large bowl, mix together the ricotta and 1 tablespoon of parsley. Slice the eggplants lengthwise into ¾ to 1-inch-thick pieces. Dredge the eggplant slices in the flour.

Coat the bottom of a large skillet with olive oil and set over medium heat. Dip the eggplant slices into the beaten egg and fry until golden brown. Add more oil as needed between batches. Drain on paper towels.

To assemble the eggplant rolls, pat the eggplant slices dry with paper towels to absorb excess oil. Place a slice of mozzarella in the middle of an eggplant slice, and top with a scoop of ricotta. Roll up the eggplant slice and place the roll, seam-side down, in greased shallow 8 x 11-inch baking pan. Repeat with the remaining eggplant slices and cheese. Pour the marinara sauce over the rolls. Bake for 15 to 20 minutes, until browned. If desired, garnish with the grated Parmesan cheese and chopped parsley.

Serves 6

Alleva Dairy's storefront (courtesy of Alleva Dairy)

Alleva Dairy's delivery truck, circa 1908 (courtesy of Alleva Dairy)

Caffé Roma

385 Broome Street, New York City

In 1891, Ronca Brothers Pastry Shop opened on the corner of Broome and Mulberry Street in New York's Little Italy. By 1952, Buddy and Vincent Zeccardi, employees in the bakery, purchased the shop and changed the name to Caffé Roma. Aside from new tables and chairs, the café, originally built in 1871, has been left unchanged. At 7:30 in the morning the dedicated bakers, some of whom have worked at the shop for decades, begin baking their cannolis, sfogliattella (the process takes six days!), biscotti, and panettone. What is truly unique is that the recipes date back 60 to 70 years and everything is baked on premises without preservatives or margarine. Only the freshest eggs, butter, and milk are used to make their popular desserts.

Caffé Roma first became well-known when Enrico Caruso, after his opera performances, would visit so he could enjoy smoking and coffee late into the night. Later, Roma became the haunt of Frank Sinatra (who is said to have ordered pignoli cookies) and numerous other celebrities, including Donna Sommers, Beverly Sills, Leonard Nimoy, Richard Dreyfuss, and Elizabeth Taylor with husbands Michael Todd and Eddie Fisher. Jacqueline Onassis would visit with her entourage and dine on cookies and espresso in the back office. The draw for

celebrities is due in part to owner Buddy Zeccardi, who provides complete privacy, making Caffé Roma a welcome and safe haven. Presently, many current television shows and commercials are filmed in there, as Caffé Roma's backdrop typifies a classic Italian café. Caffé Roma's reputation for tradition is well earned. It is simply the most authentic Italian coffee house in New York City.

Caffé Roma's Cannoli Filling

16 ounces (2 cups) ricotta impastata cheese or drained regular ricotta

1 cup sugar

½ tablespoon pure vanilla

8 ounces chocolate chips

2 tablespoons finely chopped candied melon or candied orange rind

12 to 15 cannoli shells

Confectioners' sugar, for dusting

To make the filling: Mix together the cheese, sugar, and vanilla in a bowl until completely blended. Fold in the chocolate chips. The filling may be stored in the refrigerator for a few days before using.

Just before serving, fill a pastry bag (or a large plastic bag with one corner cut) with the cheese mixture and fill the shells. Dust with the confectioners' sugar.

Serves 12 to 15

> **Tip:** When filling a cannoli, Caffé Roma suggests fill it partway from one end, and then turn the shell around and finish filling it from the other end.

Diners at Caffé Roma, circa 1955 (courtesy of Brian Merlis)

Grotta Azzurra

177 Mulberry Street, New York City

The Grotta Azzurra on Mulberry Street, in New York City's Little Italy, has been a lesson in Italian "renaissance." It has been transformed from a basement grotto that served as a secret hideaway, with a private entrance and discreet stairwells for celebrities like Jackie Kennedy Onassis and Frank Sinatra as well as many politicians, to a newly furbished and remodeled five-star restaurant.

Founded in 1908 by the Davino family, the name, G. Davino, still shines on the neon sign that lights the street. The famed Wine Room has served the locals and tourists for years. However, in 1997, the restaurant fell on hard times, as many of the restaurants did in this area, and was forced to close. But, luckily for Little Italy, a descendant of the Davino family reinvented this classic and it was reopened in September 2003 with the same Old World recipes that were handed down from father to son since the 1800s.

A restored mural of the old Grotta, named for the blue grotto on the little island of Capri, is now at the entrance to the kitchen and the color of the sea, the blue grotto, is evident throughout.

(courtesy of Grotta Azzurra)

Dining room and wine cellar at Grotta Azzura (courtesy of Grotta Azzurra)

Grotta Azzurra's Steak Pizzaiola

Two 1-inch-thick rib-eye steaks (about 1 pound)
1 tablespoon plus 1 teaspoon extra-virgin olive oil
1 tablespoon chopped garlic
1 (14-ounce) can crushed Italian tomatoes, drained
1½ teaspoons salt
Dash of black pepper
¼ teaspoon dried oregano
Chopped fresh parsley, for garnish

Heat 1 tablespoon of the olive oil in a heavy skillet over high heat. When the oil is hot, add the garlic and cook until golden brown, about 2 minutes. Add the tomatoes, salt, pepper, and oregano. Increase the heat to high and cook for 10 minutes.

In another skillet, heat the remaining 1 teaspoon of oil over high heat and sear the steak for 4 minutes on each side for medium donenesss. Drain the oil from the pan and pour the tomato sauce over steak. Cook for 4 minutes over medium heat to warm the sauce and allow the flavors to mingle. Garnish with the chopped parsley.

Serves 2

Grotta

Appetizers

Antipasto	7.95	Italian Style Salami	8.00
Pimentos and Anchovies	7.95	Celery and Olives	5.50
Filet of Anchovies	7.95	Shrimp Cocktail	7.95
Prosciutto	8.50	Fresh Mozzarella with or without Sundried Tomato, Roasted Peppers	

Hot Appetizers

Clams Oreganata	7.50	Shrimps French Style	14.95
Zuppa Di Clams, Red and White	8.95	Shrimps alla Marinara	14.95
Zuppa Di Mussels, Red and White	8.95	Stuffed Mushrooms	6.95
Shrimps-Oreganata	14.95	Spedini alla Romana	8.75
Boiled Artichokes		Stuffed Pepper	
Stuffed Artichokes			

Soups

Minestrone	4.25	Spinach	4.25
Consomme	3.25	Pavese	4.25
Consomme with Pastina	4.25	Egg Drop with Pastina	4.25
Egg Drop	4.25	Pasta E Fagioli	6.50
Escarole	4.25		

Pastas

House Special: Al Filetto Di Pomodoro, Putanesca, Carbonara

Spaghetti alla Grotta Azzurra	11.95	Tortellini	9.95
Spaghetti, Butter Sauce	7.50	Ziti, Sicilian Style	11.95
Spaghetti, Garlic, Oil and Anchovies	11.95	Ziti, Clam Sauce	11.95
Spaghetti, Garlic and Oil	11.75	Ziti, Meat Sauce	11.95
Spaghetti, Clam Sauce (White or Red)	11.95	Linguini, Clam Sauce	11.95
Spaghetti, Marinara Sauce	11.95	Linguini, Mussel Sauce	11.95
Spaghetti, Meat Sauce	11.95	Home Made Fettuccine	11.95
Spaghetti, Tomato Sauce	11.95	Home Made Cheese Ravioli	9.95
Spaghetti, Mushroom Sauce	11.95	Home Made Manicotti	9.95
Spaghetti, Sicilian Style	11.95	Gnocchi	9.95
Spaghetti, Meat Ball	11.95	Extra Sauce	1.50

Steaks and Chops

Steak Contadino with Peppers, Mushrooms, Potato	20.95	Lamb Chops, Broiled	20.95
Lamb Chops, Pizzaiola	20.95	Broiled Steak	19.95
Pork Chops, Broiled	17.95	Steak Pizzaiola	20.95
Pork Chops, Pizzaiola	19.95	Sicilian Steak	19.95
		Peppered Steak	20.95

Seafood

Calamari, Any Style	13.95	Whiting, Livornese	14.95
Mixed Fried Fish (Frittomisto)	13.95	Whiting, Boiled	12.95
Red Snapper, Broiled	19.95	Whiting, Fried	12.95
Red Snapper, Grotta Azzurra Style	19.95	Whiting, Grotta Azzurra Style	18.95
(with Calamari, Clam, Mussel, Onion, White Sauce)		(with Calamari, Clam, Mussel, Onions, White Sauce)	
Scungili Marinara	14.95	Red Snapper, Livornese	18.95
Zuppa Di Pesce	18.95	Shrimps Parmigiana	14.95
Seafood Platter (with Clams, Shrimps, Mussels, Calamari)	42.95	Octopus	

Maine Lobster

Lobster Fra Diacolo	Broiled	
Broiled Drawn Butter	Oreganata	
Lobster Arraggista		

According to the Size

Azzurra

Entrees

Chicken Rollatine Grotta Azzurra ... 16.95

Chicken, Garlic, Vinegar and Olive Oil	11.95	Veal Piccata	17.95
Chicken, Scarpariello	11.95	Veal Chop Parmigiana	19.95
Chicken, French Style	14.95	Saltimbocca alla Florentina	18.95
Chicken, Parmigiana	15.95	Sausage-Contadino (with Peppers, Mushrooms, Potato)	16.95
Chicken, alla Caterina	14.95	Sausage Pizzaiola (with Pepper and Mushrooms)	16.95
Half Chicken, Contadino	16.95	Pork Chop Parmigiana	18.95
(with Peppers, Mushrooms, Potato)		Beef Braciole and Vegetable	16.95
Half Chicken, Parmigiana	14.95	Meatball Parmigiana	10.95
Chicken, Steak and Sausage Contadino	42.95	Meat Balls and Vegetables	14.95
(with Peppers, Mushrooms, Potato)		Eggplant Parmigiana	11.50
Veal Scaloppine with Peppers and Mushrooms	16.95	Tripe	14.95
Veal Scallopine, alla Marsala	16.95	Calves Liver, Venetian	16.95
Veal Scallopine, French Style	16.95	Calves Liver, Saute Garlic & Oil	15.95
Veal Cutlet alla Parmigiana	16.95	Chicken Liver Saute with or without Mushrooms	16.95
Veal Rollatine al Marsala with Mushroom	16.95	Calves Brains, Au Gratin	11.95
Veal Spezzatino and Mushroom and Peppers	16.95	Calves Brains, Butter Sauce	11.95
Veal Cutlet, Milanese	11.95	Calves Brains, Milanese Style	11.95
Veal Pizzaiola	17.95	Veal Kidney and Mushrooms	11.50
		Veal Kidney, Broiled	10.95

Fresh Vegetables In Season

Broccoli, Any Style	6.75	Spinach, Saute	6.25
Broccoli Rape	11.50	Peppers, Fritt'	6.25
Escarole, Saute	6.25	Mushrooms alla Marinara	6.25
		Peppers, Sweet and Sour	6.25

Assorted Frys

Mixed Fried Vegetables (Frittomisto)	13.95	Potato Croquettes	4.95
Spedini alla Romana	8.75	Rice Croquettes	4.95
Mozzarella in Carrozza	8.75	Zucchini Fritti	7.50
German Fried Potatoes	4.95	Patate Fritti	3.95
Julienne Potatoes	4.95		

Salads

Mixed Green Salad	4.50	Sliced Tomatoes	4.25
House Salad	5.75		

Desserts

Biscuit Tortoni	3.00	Cold Zambaglion with Strawberry	4.95
Spumoni	3.00	Italian Cheese Cake	4.95
Tartufo	4.95	Fresh Fruit In Season	

Beverages

American Coffee	2.00	Demi Tasse	2.00
Soda	2.00	Tea	2.00
Imported Beer	3.95	Beer, Bottle Only	3.50

Menu (courtesy of Grotta Azzurra)

Grotta Azzurra's Chicken Cacciatore

1 cup extra-virgin olive oil

1 whole 3½ to 4-pound chicken, cut into 12 pieces

½ medium onion, chopped

2 cups sliced fresh mushrooms

⅔ cup white wine

5 slices Italian prosciutto

2 tablespoons butter

2 cups chicken broth

1 teaspoon chopped fresh parsley

Dash of freshly ground black pepper

Heat the oil in a large skillet over high heat. When the oil is hot add the chicken and brown. When chicken is almost cooked (the juices should run clear when the flesh is pierced), add the onion and cook until the onion is translucent, about 5 minutes. Add the mushrooms and cook for another 5 minutes, until the mushrooms are softened. Drain the oil from the pan and add the white wine, prosciutto, and butter. Cook for about 10 minutes. Add the chicken broth, parsley, and pepper. Simmer over medium heat until the sauce thickens, about 10 minutes.

Serves 4

Grotta Azzurra's Lentil Soup

1 pound lentils

3 quarts water

3 tablespoons extra-virgin olive oil

2 cloves garlic, chopped

2 celery stalks, chopped

2 slices prosciutto

½ cup crushed tomatoes

¼ cup diced salt pork

Salt and pepper, to taste

Basil, to taste

Wash the lentils and place in a large stockpot with the water. Bring to a boil, and then reduce the heat to low.

In a skillet, heat the olive oil over high heat. Brown the garlic in the hot oil. (Watch carefully as it burns quickly.) Immediately add the celery, prosciutto, and tomatoes, and reduce the heat to low. Simmer for 2 minutes.

Add the tomato mixture to the pot with the lentils. Stir to combine and cook over low heat for about 1½ to 2 hours.

Serves 4 to 6

(courtesy of Grotta Azzurra)

Puglia Restaurant

189 Hester Street, New York City

Puglia is one of the oldest restaurants in New York City's Little Italy, and it hasn't changed much at all. This family-run restaurant, now in its third-generation, looks no different than it did the day it opened.

In 1919, Gregorio Garofalo emigrated from Puglia, in Southern Italy, to realize his American dream. With a knowledge of creating homemade wines and a passion for cooking, Garofalo rented a tiny basement on Mott Street in the Little Italy section of New York City, put in coal stoves, and sprinkled sawdust on the floor. His dream of serving Italian "soul food" had begun. In 1947, in the new Hester Street location, Puglia operated without a menu or a cash register. Gregorio never used advertising to promote the restaurant, instead relying on his good customer base and "word of mouth." The friendly atmosphere of Puglia, true to its slogan "Vero Ritrovo Familari," meaning "it's a friendly place to be," would always bring customers back.

The special dishes that Gregorio prepared were considered peasant food by many, but were long-time favorites of the locals who knew they could count on finding their native dishes at Puglia. Capuzello (sheep's head) and tripe (the lining of the stomach of a young ox) were considered a delicacy, and Puglia was the place to find them. That was then and today, though the sheep's heads are gone, the character of the place is still warm and lively. It's a bit like an Italian wedding with an in-house band, music blasting, people singing, waiters yelling, and plates flying! The tables are communal, so, if you don't like the group you're with, you can always join others at another table. You can bet if they're tourists, they will welcome you.

Puglia Ristorante

In The Heart of Little Italy
Established 1919

In 1919 Gregorio Garofalo, came over from Italy to begin his American dream . . . he rented a basement, put in his coal stoves, and sprinkled saw dust on the floor. With his knowledge of creating homemade wines and his passion for cooking, Gregorio's dream began . . . . .

The name... "Puglia" a region in Southern Italy, from which he immigrated. People came from far, to indulge in the delicacies Gregorio prepared. Capuzzello (sheepshead), Tripe (the lining of the stomach of a young ox) Pasta E. Fagioli (pasta with beans) but what they loved the most, was the way he treated everyone like his own family.

Today with his 3rd generation carrying on the recipes & values he taught them, Gregorio is smiling...all of us at Puglia, thank you for making Gregorio's dream a reality.

. . . . Buona Sera

189 Hester Street • Little Italy
New York City
Tel: 212-966-6006 • Fax: 212-966-6033
Music Nightly

Menu cover (courtesy of Puglia Restaurant)

Puglia's Filetto di Pomodoro

1 (35-ounce) can Italian plum tomatoes,
    lightly crushed by hand

5 tablespoons extra-virgin olive oil

1 medium onion, chopped

⅓ pound prosciutto, chopped

3 fresh basil leaves, chopped

Salt and black pepper, to taste

⅓ cup water

1 pound dried penne pasta

Heat the olive oil in large skillet over medium heat. Add the onion and prosciutto and sauté until the onion is clear and the prosciutto is browned. Crush the tomatoes and add them, with their juice, to the pan. Mix in the basil, salt, pepper, and water. Simmer over low heat for 15 minutes. While the sauce is cooking, cook the penne pasta in a large pot of boiling salted water according to package directions. Drain the pasta well and add to the sauce. Mix gently and serve.

Serves 4

Puglia's Veal Picatta

1 pound veal, thinly sliced

4 tablespoons flour

Pinch of salt and pepper

3 ounces (¾ stick) butter

½ cup beef broth

⅓ cup white wine

Juice ½ lemon

2 tablespoons minced freshly parsley
    plus 1 sprig fresh parsley

1 lemon slice

Pound the veal slices until they are about ⅛-inch thick. In a shallow bowl, mix together the flour, salt, and pepper. Dredge the veal in the flour mixture.

Melt the butter in a large skillet over low heat. When melted, increase the heat to high and brown the veal in the butter on both sides. Transfer the veal to a serving dish and cover.

Return the pan to medium-high heat. Add the beef broth and white wine, bring to a boil, and then reduce by half over low heat, stirring occasionally to deglaze the pan and loosen

Menu (courtesy of Puglia Restaurant)

the browned bits from the pan. Remove the pan from the heat and stir in the lemon juice and minced parsley. Pour the sauce over the meat and serve. Garnish with the lemon slice and parsley sprig.

Serves 2

Lombardi's Pizza

32 Spring Street, New York City

New York City pizza is the pizza by which all others are judged. That was the case when Generoso Lombardi put New York City pizza on the map, and it still is today!

In 1897, young and barely able to speak English, Generoso, who had immigrated to the United States from Naples in 1895, opened a grocery store in the heart of Little Italy. There he sold bread topped with tomatoes to the local immigrants on their way to work in the factories and subways of New York City. He would wrap this first "pizza" in brown paper and tie it closed with string. The men would warm their tomato-topped bread on hot coals when ready to eat. His store was well-known to the local immigrants and, through his influence in the community, he helped those who were out of work to obtain jobs.

In 1905, at 53½ Spring Street, in the now legendary Little Italy of New York, Lombardi's Pizza was born. The entire Lombardi family worked in the restaurant where originally there was only one kind of pizza offered and only one style of dough. Generoso began to top the "pies" with mozzarella cheese, and, with this innovation, his became the first licensed pizzeria in America. If you wanted to make pizza, sell pizza, or know anything about

pizza, you came to Generoso Lombardi. He was the expert and the teacher to all who aspired to attain this knowledge. Lombardi's was a popular hangout for entertainers and most especially for Enrico Caruso, who ate at Lombardi's at least once a week. Legend has it that John Brescio, Sr., the father of the current co-owner, heard him sing so loud one night that he shattered a glass.

Over time, the vibration from the subway that runs underneath 53½ Spring Street caused the brick oven to crumble. Along with the loss of the oven, the economic downturn in 1986 forced the restaurant to close.

Tossing the pizza dough (courtesy of Lombardi's Pizza)

John Brescio and the unearthed coal-fired oven (courtesy of Lombardi's Pizza)

But, in 1994, John Brescio and his childhood friend, Gennaro, the grandson of Generoso Lombardi, joined together to re-open the famed pizza restaurant just a few doors to the east at 32 Spring Street, which was at one time an old bread bakery. To their amazement, behind a wall remained a perfectly intact coal-fired brick oven. With the help of some Italian masons, the bricks were dug out and the oven was re-built. A steady 900-degree temperature was necessary for two weeks in order for the bricks to cure. Due to the high heat it produces, it is no longer permitted to build a coal-fired oven in a restaurant, but to unearth one that can be salvaged is a rare discovery.

Other than the addition of the large Hobart dough machine, not much has changed at Lombardi's. There is not much to do: just keep it simple, keep it fresh, and keep it crisp. It is an undisputable fact that this century-old method of pizza making gives the pizza a unique, crisp, slightly burnt crust that takes a mere 3½ minutes to bake. People come from all over the world to eat here, and now John Brescio's son Mike has joined his father at the helm of this world-renowned landmark. This is Little Italy at its best!

(courtesy of Lombardi's Pizza)

Lombardi's first pizzeria on Spring Street (courtesy of Lombardi's Pizza)

The current location of Lombardi's (courtesy of Lombardi's Pizza)

Lombardi's Grandma Grace's Meatball Recipe

1 cup grated Pecorino Romano cheese

1 teaspoon granulated garlic, preferably McCormick's®

½ cup Italian-style bread crumbs

1 tablespoon fresh ground black pepper

4 tablespoons chopped fresh parsley

1 tablespoon salt

2 pounds ground beef

4 eggs

Extra-virgin olive oil, for frying

In a small bowl, mix together the cheese, granulated garlic, breadcrumbs, black pepper, parsley, and salt by hand until well combined.

In a large bowl, mix together the beef and eggs. When well mixed, start adding the cheese mixture, a little at a time, and mix by hand or in a food processor just until everything is incorporated. It is extremely important not to over mix the meat. (The total mixing time should be no more than 15 seconds if using a mixer or food processor.)

Using your hands, roll the mixture into meatballs 1½-inches in diameter.

In a large skillet, pour enough oil just to coat the bottom of the pan. Heat the oil over medium-high heat. When hot, fry

the meatballs until brown, about 15 to 18 minutes. Drain meatballs on paper towels. The meatballs can be served in a tomato sauce with spaghetti or as an appetizer with a dipping sauce of your choice. If serving in a tomato sauce, place 4 cups of the tomato sauce of your choice in a large saucepan. Gently add the meatballs and let them warm on medium heat for 15 minutes.

Makes 10 to 12 (4-ounce) meatballs

Lombardi's Grandma Grace's New York Style Cheese Cannoli

Cannoli Shells

8 cups flour

1 tablespoon baking powder

4 cups sugar (see note on next page)

4 ounces (1 stick) unsalted butter, softened

6 eggs

2 tablespoons vanilla extract

Special tools

Pizelle iron, cannoli forms, pastry bag with rosette tip

Cheese Filling

1 pound ricotta impastata cheese or drained regular ricotta (see tip on next page)

1½ cups confectioners' sugar

1 tablespoon pure vanilla extract

Melted milk chocolate or chocolate chips, as you prefer

(courtesy of Mario's Restaurant)

if they have since moved away, still return to shop in the same places that their families have always done. The pace is slow and the merchants treat every customer as if he or she was a long-lost cousin. The sights and sounds, and most especially the aromas, of this quintessential Italian neighborhood are a delight to experience. The air is perfumed with the scents of freshly baked breads and pastries, spicy, freshly made sausages, fried calamari, and the veritable red sauces made each day that waft from the windows of the restaurant kitchens.

The Belmont section of the Bronx, home to one of the best Little Italys in America, isn't going anywhere . . . thankfully.

Be prepared to fall in love.

Artuso Pastry

670 East 187th Street, Bronx

Artuso Store front circa 1968 (courtesy of Artuso Pastry)

Italian guilt, family pressure — call it what you may, but it is a good thing. It is what keeps one generation after another together, working and building for the future. As in so many Italian businesses in the Little Italy communities in America, the younger generations have invariably become educated, but many have then felt the call of the family trade. In an effort to keep the family together, each generation was not willing to lose what their grandparents or even their great grandparents came to America to build.

Artuso Pastry shop and the Artuso family are a prime example of this tradition.

Vincent F. Artuso, Sr. emigrated from Reggio di Calabria in 1930 with his brother Jack and sister Anna. Though just children at the time, it was the Depression and so they had to find a means to help support their family. Not happy with his job building shoeshine boxes, Vincent began an apprenticeship at Spagnola's Pastry Shop in the neighborhood. He knew he had found his calling. After WWII he married his wife, Betty, and together they purchased Spagnola's Pastry Shop and never looked back. A beloved figure on Arthur Avenue, there is now a street named for him on the corner of East 187th Street and Cambreleng Avenue.

Today the pastry shop has a wholesale division run by the Artuso's grandson, Anthony Jr., who, though armed with a business degree, decided that family ties were more important than wearing a tie to work every day. Their granddaughter, Connie Artuso, takes care of the business side of the bakery and, because of their efforts, they have become a cannoli-producing powerhouse!

Aunt Anna still makes the pastries and, along with the scrumptious cannolis, sfogliatelle, tiramisu, and biscotti, they also have the best house-made Italian ices.

And the people keep coming. Those who grew up here and moved away still come to shop and tourists always come for the bread and pastries. This shop, and others like it, are evidence that Arthur Avenue is the closest thing to Italy this side of the Atlantic.

Julie M., Anthony, Sr., and Patty M. at the pastry case (courtesy of Artuso Pastry)

Artuso's Anginette Cookies

4 cups all-purpose flour

2 teaspoons baking powder

½ teaspoon salt

8 ounces (2 sticks) unsalted butter

½ cup sugar

6 eggs

1 teaspoon pure vanilla extract

Icing

2 tablespoons milk

2 teaspoons pure vanilla extract

2 (1-lb) boxes confectioners' sugar

Sugar, preferably decorating sugar
(also called sugar crystals), for garnish (see note)

Preheat the oven to 375°F.

In a bowl, mix together the flour, baking powder, and salt. Set aside.

In a large mixing bowl, cream the butter, and then, while beating, gradually add the sugar. Continue beating until fluffy. Add eggs and vanilla extract; cream well. Add the dry ingredients and mix until dough has a smooth texture — like a butter cookie. Chill the dough until firm.

Drop the dough the heaping teaspoon onto a cookie sheet and bake for 10 minutes, or until light brown.

To make the icing: Beat the ingredients together with an electric mixer until you have a medium-thick consistency. Brush the icing on the cookies and sprinkle on the sugar. Store the cookies at room temperature for up to 3 weeks.

Note: Decorating sugar, also known as coarse sugar, sugar crystals, or crystal sugar, is about four times larger than regular granulated sugar. It can be found at cake-decorating stores or gourmet shops.

Makes 50 cookies

Artuso's famous selection of Italian cookies in the original display case (courtesy of Artuso Pastry)

Artuso's Pignoli Cookies

¾ cup plus 2 tablespoons sugar

1 pound almond paste

3 egg whites

½ cup plus 1 tablespoon pignoli nuts (pine nuts)

Preheat the oven to 350°F.

Beat the almond paste and sugar in a food processor until the texture becomes crumbly. Put the almond mixture in a large bowl and add the egg whites. Stir until well blended. Working with 1 teaspoon of dough at a time, roll the dough into medium-sized balls using your fingertips. Roll each ball in the pignoli nuts.

Line a cookie sheet with parchment (or grocery bags). Do not grease the pans. Place the place balls 2 inches apart on the prepared cookies sheets. Bake for 15 minutes. The cookie is done when the center is firm to the touch. Make sure the cookies have cooled completely before removing them from the parchment or they will crumble. Store in the refrigerator for 1 to 1½ weeks or freeze up to 3 months.

Makes 35 cookies

Artuso's Anisette Biscotti

4 ounces (1 stick) unsalted butter
5 eggs
4 cups all-purpose flour
3 teaspoons baking powder
¾ cup plus 2 tablespoons sugar
½ teaspoon salt
2 ounces anisette or 2 teaspoons anise extract

Preheat the oven to 350°F.

In a large mixing bowl, cream the butter, and then, while beating, gradually add the sugar. Continue beating until fluffy. Add the eggs, one at a time, beating well after each addition. Sift in the dry ingredients and add the anisette; mix well.

Shape into 4 loaves and place on a lightly greased cookie sheet. Bake for 35 minutes, or until the top and bottom are golden brown. When baked, remove from the oven and immediately place on a cutting board. (Leave the oven on.)

Cut into ½-inch slices. Place the slices cut-side up on an ungreased baking sheet and toast in the oven for 7 minutes on each side. Be sure to turn the biscotti over to ensure they are evenly toasted. Remove, cool, and serve with coffee, espresso, or cappuccino.

Makes 47 biscotti

Artuso's Cannoli Cream Filling

3 teaspoons sugar
1 teaspoons pure vanilla extract
1½ teaspoons ground cinnamon
12 ounces (1½ cups) ricotta impastata cheese or drained regular ricotta

In a bowl, beat all of the ingredients together with an electric mixer until smooth and creamy. Chill until ready to use. (It will keep for a few days in the refrigerator.) This can be used as a filling for cannoli shells, pastry shells, or cakes.

Fills 7 to 10 cannoli shells

Street sign honoring Vincent F. Artuso Sr. (courtesy of Artuso Pastry)

Artuso's authentic pignoli cookies (courtesy of Artuso Pastry)

Borgatti's Ravioli & Egg Noodles

632 East 187th Street, Bronx

On Arthur Avenue in the Bronx, there are a myriad of small, family-owned stores, all doing what they do extremely well. Many offer fresh meats, cheeses, fresh fish, or pastry, but at Borgatti's, the proprietors have a particularly special niche, rarely found even in this stronghold of proud, ethnic eats.

In 1899, Lindo Borgatti emigrated from Bologna, Italy to Boston, where he met and married his wife, Maria, in 1907. After working for the Pastene Company in Boston, he transferred to the Pastene warehouse in Greenwich Village in New York City. By 1915, Lindo and Maria moved to the Arthur Avenue section of the Bronx. There Lindo worked as a retail grocer before opening his own small store on 187th Street, and it remains in the same location to this day.

It was in the depths of the Depression, in 1935, when Lindo Borgatti, while suffering from rheumatic fever, began to make egg noodles and ravioli to sell in his new store. The ravioli was made by hand on a grooved wooden board using a hand press and double rollers to cut the ravioli. By 1947, Borgatti's progressed to a newer, more modern ravioli machine. The antique "noodle cutter" is still present as a reminder of how things used to be in Borgatti's. They continue to use only eggs, water, and durum wheat flour for their pasta. This combination makes a much stronger dough that cannot be extruded into the many pasta shapes that are commonly made with semolina flour.

The only pasta that Borgatti's sells is flat egg noodles, though various sizes and widths can be chosen from a tattered cardboard chart painted with yellow stripes. The pasta can become lasagna, capellini, or anything in between, depending on the customer's preference. The egg noodles are sliced in front of the customer from fresh, one-and-a half-foot-square sheets of dough that are hand fed into the set size of bladed rollers, placed on paper, sprinkled with cornmeal to prevent sticking, and then wrapped.

(718) 367-3799

Borgatti's
Ravioli & Egg Noodles

632 East 187th Street
Bronx, NY 10458

Tues. - Sat. 9 am - 6 pm
Sunday 8 am - 1 pm
Closed Mondays

Today, Mario and his son Christopher are at the helm of this most unique Old World establishment with five generations helping in various positions at the shop. In a nod to more modern tastes, they now make dried spinach and dried tomato pasta as well as the ricotta, meat, and spinach ravioli. But it's only flat, fresh pasta that tastes like the essence of an Italian home-cooked meal.

Borgatti's Manicotti with Marinara Sauce

Marinara Sauce

(Makes 3½ quarts)

⅔ cup extra-virgin olive oil

4 cloves garlic, thinly sliced

Salt and freshly ground black pepper, to taste

4 (28-ounce) cans crushed plum tomatoes

20 fresh basil leaves, chopped (or 2 tablespoons dried)

2 tablespoons chopped fresh parsley leaves
(or 2 teaspoons dried)

Manicotti Filling

1 (48-ounce) container ricotta cheese

3 eggs

¾ cup grated Parmesan cheese

⅓ cup minced Italian (flat-leaf) parsley

Salt and pepper, to taste

24 squares fresh manicotti squares or substitute dried
pre-formed manicotti-cannelloni tubes

To make the marinara sauce: Heat the oil in a medium saucepan over medium-low heat. Add the garlic and sauté until softened. Add the remaining ingredients, increase the heat to medium-high, and bring to a simmer, stirring often.

Simmer for 30 minutes over medium-low heat. The sauce can be stored for up to 5 days in the refrigerator and several months in the freezer.

Preheat the oven to 375°F. Bring a large pot of salted water to a boil.

While the water is coming to a boil, make the manicotti filling: Combine the ricotta, eggs, Parmesan, parsley, salt, and pepper in a bowl. Set aside.

If using fresh manicotti squares, cook the fresh pasta in the boiling, salted water for just 1 minute. If using dried manicotti tubes, cook the dried pasta in the boiling, salted water according to package directions. Remove the pot from the heat, but do not drain the pasta in a colander as the squares or tubes may stick together. Instead, pour off a good portion of the hot water (but leave enough so that the pasta is still submerged under water). Then run cold water into the pot until you can fish the pasta out safely with your fingers. Shake off the excess water as you remove each square or tube. Lay the squares flat on a clean cloth and blot them dry.

Spread one ladleful of the sauce onto the bottom of a 9 x 12-inch baking pan.

To fill the squares: Place the filling across the center of one of the dough squares, leaving a little room at the edges on each side. Turn up the edge nearest you so that it lies on top of the filling. Now turn the edge farthest from you towards you so that it lies on top of the first edge. You now have a cannoli-like tube. Turn the manicotti over and place it seam-side down in the baking pan on top of the sauce. Continue until the pan has a layer of manicotti.

To fill the tubes: Using a piping bag or a small spoon, carefully stuff a pasta tube with the filling. Place the filled tube in the baking pan on top of the sauce. Continue until the pan has a layer of manicotti.

Spoon 2 more ladlefuls of sauce over the top of the filled manicotti and bake for 45 minutes. Remove from the oven and let sit 10 minutes before serving. Serve with additional sauce on the side.

Serves 12

Borgatti's Fettuccine Alfredo

1 pound fresh fettuccine noodles
6 ounces (1½ sticks) butter
½ cup heavy cream
2 ounces Parmesan cheese, grated (½ cup)
1 egg yolk
Pepper mill for freshly grinding pepper over individual servings, as desired

Cook the fettuccini in a large pot of salted boiling until al dente, about 4 to 5 minutes.

While fettuccine is cooking, melt the butter over low heat in a double boiler (or use a bowl set over a sauce pan with simmering water). Whisk in the heavy cream and half of the Parmesan cheese.

When the noodles are cooked, drain well and immediately place them in a large serving bowl. (Do not allow the noodles to sit in the drainer for long or they become dry.) Pour the hot butter sauce over the noodles, add the egg yolk and toss rapidly to cook the yolk. Serve immediately while piping hot with the remaining Parmesan cheese and freshly ground black pepper, as desired.

Serves 4

Mario Borgatti (courtesy of Borgatti's Ravioli & Egg Noodles)

Teitel Brothers

2372 Arthur Avenue, Bronx

Huge salamis hang from the ceiling, fresh mozzarella swim in vats of water, watermelon-sized wheels of Parmegiana-Reggiano sit on the crowded counter ready to be cut, and tins of tomatoes, bottles of olive oil, and jars of olives, mushrooms, beans, and nuts sit on shelves in this small, cramped bazaar-like food market. There is such an overwhelming supply of goods that during the day the cans of private-label Italian plum tomatoes, bottles of their own brand of olive oils, and the barrels of *stoccafisso* (salt cod) are displayed outside in front of the store.

The story of this immigrant family is the same as all others, except, here on Arthur Avenue, the Teitel family is not Italian, but Jewish. In a neighborhood that was 99.9 percent Italian, the Teitels set up their home and their business, and it worked just fine. Their lives became as ingrained in the neighborhood as the other immigrants of that time.

Jacob and his brother, Morris Teitel, immigrated to America from Austria before World War I, settling on Delancy Street on the Lower East Side of New York City, where they worked as tailors. When, in 1915, a store on Arthur Avenue became

(courtesy of Teitel Brothers)

available, the brothers moved to the Bronx and opened Teitel Brothers market. They all lived together in the same apartment above the market, and it was there that Jacob and his wife raised their three sons. In those pre-Depression and pre-refrigeration days, goods were delivered by horse and wagon. When the store was too busy to handle all of its customers, Jacob Teitel would bang on the pipes for his wife to come down to assist.

In an effort to accommodate the locals, Jacob Teitel, an Orthodox Jew, would keep his market open for business on the Sabbath, which was unheard of for such a pious man. During the Depression a mosaic Star of David was embedded in the entrance of their market as a statement against the Fascism that was raging throughout Europe. In 1957, Teitel Brothers went into the wholesale business to accommodate its growing customer base, but the family keeps up the old traditions, and is ever-present to serve customers.

The store is now run by Gil Teitel and two of his three sons, Michael and Edward. This third-generation family-run and family-oriented business is proud to have served Governors Mario Cuomo, Hugh Carrey, and George Pataki, Senator Hillary Clinton, and scores of celebrities, such as former resident and quintessential Italian actor, Joe Pesci. It might seem odd that this authentic Italian grocery, in the most Italian of the Little Italys in America, is run by non-Italians. But isn't this what the melting-pot immigrant experience is all about?

Gil Teitel (courtesy of Teitel Brothers)

Teitel Brothers Baccalà Napolitano

⅓ pound dried salt cod fillet (baccalà)

¾ cup rich chicken stock, preferably Knorrs® chicken base

1 cup extra-virgin olive oil, preferably EDDA®

1 onion, preferably Spanish, sliced

1 red bell pepper, stemmed, deseeded, and julienned

1 yellow bell pepper, stemmed, deseeded, and julienned

1 (28-ounce) can whole, peeled Italian plum tomatoes, drained, preferably Francesconi SanManzano®

½ cup white wine

2 Idaho potatoes, peeled and cut into ½-inch wedges

5 cloves garlic, smashed with the side of large knife and chopped

Dash of freshly ground black pepper

¼ teaspoon sea salt

Marinara Sauce

⅓ cup extra-virgin olive oil, preferably EDDA®

4 cloves garlic, smashed with the side of a large knife

1 (28-ounce) can whole, peeled Italian tomatoes, preferably Francesconi SanManzano®, drained

Dash of dried oregano

4 to 5 leaves fresh basil, torn from stem with fingers

½ teaspoon sea salt

Dash of black pepper

Variations to add flair:

1 teaspoon capers

Handful of pitted, oven-cured olives

Handful of pitted Cerignola olives

Handful of pitted Castelvetrano olives

Lay the cod on cutting board. Cut the filet into 2½-inch pieces. Let the fish soak in a bowl of cold water in the refrigerator for 4 days, changing the water twice a day.

When the dried cod is ready to be used, make the marinara sauce. In a large saucepan, heat the ⅓ cup of olive oil over low heat. Add the garlic and sauté until golden, about 2 minutes. (Be careful not to burn the garlic.) Add the tomatoes, oregano, basil, salt and pepper to the pan. Simmer for 20 minutes. Set aside. (**Note:** the marinara sauce can be made 2 to 3 days ahead and kept in refrigerator for 3 to 4 days.)

Preheat the oven to 450°F.

If using chicken stock prepared with the Knorrs® chicken base, bring ¾ cup of water to a boil in a saucepan with 1 teaspoon of the chicken base, stirring until the chicken base is dissolved. Set aside.

In a large saucepan, heat ⅓ cup of the olive oil over medium heat. Add the onion, red and yellow peppers, and capers or olives, if using, and sauté until carmelized and golden, about 2 minutes. Add the white wine, chicken stock, and marinara sauce and simmer for 3 minutes.

In a large skillet, heat the remaining ⅔ cup of olive oil over medium-high heat. Add the potatoes, garlic, salt, and pepper and sauté for 10 minutes until brown on all sides.

Place the filets of baccalà in a 9 x12-inch glass baking dish. Top with the potatoes and one-half of the bell pepper sauce.

Bake, covered, for 1 hour, at 450° until fish flakes with a fork. Remove from the oven, let sit for 5 to 10 minutes before serving. Spoon juices from the fish into remaining pepper sauce. Simmer the pepper sauce briefly, pour over the fish and serve with saffron rice or garlic-mashed potatoes.

Serves 2 to 4

TEITEL BROS. Inc.

2372 Arthur Ave., Cor. 186th St. — Bronx, N. Y.

"The Big Corner Store"

Tel. SEdgwick 3-4168

Deliveries to all parts of the City and Westchester

25th ANNIVERSARY SALE

KIRKMAN OCTAGON CLEANSER 3¢ each	CRISAFULLI 1.75	PASTENE COFFEE .... 24¼¢ lb.
P. & G. SOAP 3 for 9¢	SQUISITA OIL 1.79	ROMA COFFEE .... 24¢ lb.
BUDDY CLEANSER 2¢ can	LA GUSTOSA OIL 80¢	MAXWELL COFFEE .... 23¢ lb.
LARGE GREEN OLIVES 3 lbs. 25¢	SUPERFINE OIL 80¢	FANCY LOOSE COFFEE .... 13¢ lb.
COBO PEAS 9¢	GREEN LUCCA 95¢	AMERICAN COFFEE (Loose - Best) 15¢ lb.
BRIOSCHI 42¢	NAPOLI OIL 95¢	MEDALIA D'ORO COFFEE .... 26¼¢ lb.
PASTENE TOMATOES WITH SAUCE Large - 19¢	PULCELLA FINE OIL 89¢	TUNA FISH PASTENE .... 8¢ can
COBO TOMATOES	TRE STELLA OLIVE OIL 2.09	TUNA FISH IN PURE OLIVE OIL 6¼
ZELO TOMATOES 13¢	FRANCESCANI OLIVE OIL 2.09	PEAS .... 5¢ can
PALADINO MACARONI BY CASE 20 lbs. 99¢	D'ANNUNZIO SALAMI (All Pork) 30¢ lb.	RIPE OLIVES IN CANS .... 10¢
LARD (Thick) 8¢ lb.	GENOA SALAMI 37¢ lb.	SALMON Large Cans 10¢
CAPOCOLLI 33¢ lb.	SOPRESSATE (Italian Style) 37¢ lb.	S A R D I N E S Large Cans - 10¢
RAMAZZOTTI 85¢ bot	PROSCIUTTO Whole Piece 29¢ lb.	THREE TREES PEAS 2 for 23¢
CARUSO TOMATOES Large 13¢	**FREE! FREE!**	SWEET PEPPERS IN JARS 12¢ jar
BLUE STAR OLIVE OIL 1.79	5 LBS. OF SUGAR WITH EVERY GAL. OF LOOSE OIL	CALIFORNIA SAUCE 6 for 25¢
THREE TREES OLIVE OIL 1.80	SALSICCE FORTE 30¢ lb.	GENUINE LOCATELLA .... 49¢ lb.
MOOSALINA OLIVE OIL 1.79 gal.	PROVOLONCINE 18¢ lb.	GENUINE ROMANO .... 45¢ lb.
BALBO OIL 87¢	BEST LOOSE MACARONI 8¢ lb.	PECORINO ROMANO .... 35¢ lb.
GEMMA OIL 87¢	LA ROSA RONZONI 3 pkgs. 22¢	PROVOLLONE AURICCHIO .... 36¢ lb.
CONTANDINA OIL 75¢	DOMINO SUGAR 5 lbs. 22¢	PROVOLONICI 18¼¢ lb.
PALMA OIL 87¢	RINSO Large 17¢	VERY OLD PARMIGIANO 49¢
B BRAND OIL 67¢	OXYDOL Large 17¢	PICKLES IN JARS 9¢
CAPATANO OIL 55¢	O. K. SOAP 4 for 10¢	KIRKMAN SOAP 7 pcs. 25¢
PASTENE OIL 1.99	LUIGI VITELLI TOMATO SAUCE 6¢	OCTAGON SOAP 7 pcs. 25¢
PHILIP BERIO 1.99	FAGIOLI CANNELLINI -- THE BEST 9¢ lb.	PALMOLIVE SOAP 5¢
BERTOLLI OIL 1.99	RED BOW LENTILS 8¢ pkg.	LUX TOILET SOAP 5¢
LA PERLA OIL 1.99		LIFEBUOY SOAP 5¢
MADRE SICILLIA 1.99		
POPE OIL 1.99		

We reserve the right to limit quantities.   Prices subject to change without notice.

Tickets given with every purchase — redeemable for valuable gifts.

Advertising poster circa 1940 (courtesy of Teitel Brothers)

Egidio Pastry Shop

622 East 187th Street, Bronx

Sibling rivalry, greed, infidelity, and bitter feelings are what come to mind when locals speak of this pinnacle of pastry on Arthur Avenue. But, what goes on behind the scenes matters not at all when you bite into one of the best pastries around.

Suffice it to say, Egidio Pastry Shop has been the literal cornerstone of Arthur Avenue for 100 years. It all began when Pasquale Egidio, a 22-year-old Southern Italian immigrant, who would give the shop its name, came to America in 1909 by way of the Neapolitan suburb of Salerno.

EST. 1912

Egidio Pastry Shop Inc.
ITALIAN & FRENCH PASTRY
CAPPUCCINO AND ESPRESSO
WEDDING & BIRTHDAY CAKES
(718) 295-6077
FAX: (718) 295-1468

CARMELA LUCCIOLA

622 EAST 187TH ST.
BRONX, N.Y. 10458

(courtesy of Egidio Pastry Shop)

Following the dream of many Italian immigrants before him, he came to America, wife and children in tow. At first Pasquale settled in the crowded tenements on the Lower East Side of Manhattan, but eventually, with the help of a family member, he rented space for a small corner café in the Bronx.

Egidio's would soon become one of the preeminent cafés in the neighborhood. But there was much sadness surrounding one of Pasquale's daughters, Annie. She idolized her father and loved being with him. Perhaps her parents took note of that as they persuaded her to drop out of high school and work in the bakery. Annie worked there for 50 years and when her father died in 1957, she assumed the shop would finally be hers but that didn't happen and the business went to her brother instead. By 1987, Egidio's was sold to Carmela Lucciola and her ex-husband, Paolo Palombo.

Through a series of unfortunate circumstances, Paolo left the business, but Carmela is still at the bakery and is the one who is there to make sure the desserts are delicious, the cappuccino perfect, and the customers content. A gleaming pastry case runs the length of the shop filled with cheesy sfogliatelle, creamy "lobster tails," fruit tarts, éclairs, and a myriad of cookies and cannolis.

Today Egidio Pastry Shop, with the omnipresent Carmela at the helm, remains a classic Italian pasticerria and a neighborhood landmark with its roots deep in Italian tradition and customs.

Anna Egidio, her father, Pasquale, and an unknown man, circa 1920 (courtesy of Egidio Pastry Shop)

Circa 1900 (courtesy of Egidio Pastry Shop)

Egidios Bakery Quaresimali (Lenten Almond Nut Biscuits)

3 cups whole almonds

¼ cup honey

2 ounces (½ stick) unsalted butter

2 large eggs

2 cups all-purpose flour

¾ cup brown sugar

1½ teaspoons ground cinnamon

1¼ teaspoons baking powder

½ cup sugar

1 large egg beaten with 1 tablespoon water for egg wash

Preheat the oven to 375°F. Spread the almonds on a greased cookie sheet and toast them until brown. Allow the almonds to cool. Lower the oven temperature to 350°F. Reserve 2¼ cups of the almonds. Finely chop the remaining almonds.

In a large bowl, mix together the chopped almonds and the honey. In a separate bowl, cream the butter, sugars and eggs, and then add to the bowl with the almond mixture. Mix well. Add the remaining dry ingredients (flour, baking powder and cinnamon, along with the reserved almonds, and mix until the dough is well blended.

Quarter the dough and firmly press each piece into a 10 x 2-inch log. Arrange the logs 2 inches apart on a large, un-greased baking sheet. Bake in the middle of the oven until golden, about 30 minutes. Leave the oven on. Loosen the logs from the baking sheet with a metal spatula, and then transfer to a cutting board. Let cool 5 minutes. Cut the logs crosswise with a large heavy knife into ½-inch-wide slices and arrange on the baking sheet, standing upright, ¼-inch apart. Brush the logs with the egg wash. Bake the cookies in middle of the oven until golden all over with firm centers, 10 to 12 minutes. Transfer to a rack to cool completely. Biscuits will keep for up to 2 weeks in an airtight container. Do not freeze.

Makes approximately 40 biscuits

De Lillo Pastry Shop

606 East 187th Street, Bronx

Can you say savoiardi, anginetti, carcagnoli, ameretti, sfogliatelle, pignoli, quaresimale and zabaglione? These are just some of the mouthwatering pastries at this bastion of Old World pastry in the Italian section of Arthur Avenue in the Bronx.

In 1924, two brothers, Rocco and Joe Delillo, immigrants from Calabria, Italy, settled in the Belmont section of the Bronx to seek their livelihoods. Even though they did not have a baking background, they purchased and were able to operate De Lillo Pastry Shop as if they had been bakers for generations. Even at quite a young age, Joe's son, Nick, and his daughter, Rose, had become well-known in the shop, and began helping out as soon as they were able to reach the counter. Eventually, as they learned the trade, they would take over the running of the shop and continue its tradition. One of the trusted employees, Luigi Florio, became close with the family, and when Nick died, Luigi partnered with Rose and began to operate the bakery. By 1984, Rose had tired of the bakery, so Luigi bought her share of the business and partnered with his brother, Salvatore, and another trusted employee.

The owners, past and present, of De Lillo have always aimed for excellence and quality and, as a result, today, the bakery is very busy. Patrons line up outside in all kinds of weather for a taste of one of De Lillo homemade pastries that are all still made in the back of the shop.

Today Sal's three children, Giuseppina, Anthony, and Sal Jr., are now at the bakery serving some of the same loyal customers who have been coming there for generations — like Nick and Rose, they started young but by now, all three can reach the counter.

(courtesy of De Lillo Pastry Shop)

De Lillo Pastry Shop Choux Pastry

4 cups water

2 teaspoons salt

16 ounces (4 sticks) unsalted butter

4¾ cups all-purpose flour

1 quart eggs (from approximately 18 to 20 extra-large eggs)

Preheat the oven to 400°F.

Bring the water, salt, and butter to a boil in an oversized pot. Remove from the heat and add flour all at once, beating with a wooden spoon until it forms a large ball.

Pour the contents into a large mixing bowl and mix slowly with a wooden spoon to let heat escape. Begin to slowly add the eggs, one by one, beating with a paddle until the eggs are fully incorporated and the mixture is cool.

Using a pastry bag fitted with a plain tube, pipe the dough into 6-inch-long tubelike pieces onto a greased cookie sheet. Bake until golden brown, about 10 minutes. Let cool and, just before serving, fill with cannoli cream. The dough will keep in the refrigerator for several weeks. The shells, on the other hand, will become soggy 1 to 2 days after they're baked, and so should be used very soon after they're baked.

Make 24 to 36 choux pastry shells depending on size

De Lillo Pastry Shop Cannoli Cream

1 pound ricotta impastata cheese or drained regular ricotta (see page 87)

¾ cup sugar

2 teaspoons ground cinnamon

1 teaspoon pure vanilla extract

¼ cup chocolate chips

In a large bowl, mix the ricotta and sugar together on with an electric mixer on medium speed until well combined and the texture is smooth. Add the cinnamon and vanilla. Continue to mix for 2 to 3 minutes until well blended. Add the chocolate chips, a few at a time, and continue mixing until well blended.

Makes enough filling for 12 cannoli shells

De Lillo Pastry Shop Pignoli Cookies

1 pound almond paste

½ pound sugar

1 teaspoon pure vanilla extract

½ cup egg whites (about 4 eggs)

1½ cups pignoli nuts (pine nuts)

Preheat the oven to 350°F.

Place the almond paste in a large mixing bowl and allow to soften. Add the sugar slowly while beating with an electric mixer on a low speed. Add the vanilla and continue mixing until well combined. Slowly add the egg whites until the mixture is soft and has the consistency of oatmeal.

With lightly floured hands, roll the dough into 1-inch balls and place them on a lightly greased cookie sheet, making sure to space them at least 1 to 2 inches apart. Place several pignoli nuts on the top each cookie and press down slightly. Bake until golden brown, about 10 to 12 minutes. Let cool and then remove from the cookie sheet with a spatula.

Makes 20 to 25 cookies

Mario's Restaurant

2342 Arthur Avenue, Bronx

The journey to America for the Migliucci family began after Giuseppe Migliucci had his hand blown off by a firecracker. Humiliated by his loss, he traveled to Cairo and opened Egypt's first Italian restaurant. From Egypt the family immigrated to America. In 1919, Giuseppe Migliucci found a 12x50-foot empty store on Arthur Avenue large enough to hold only six small tables. It was here that the legend of Mario's began.

Mario's Restaurant, named for Giuseppe's son, first started as a pizzeria, but, as the years passed, the family expanded the original site, and it grew to be known as one of the finest restaurants for Neapolitan cooking on Arthur Avenue. The best cracker-thin pizza crust in the area is still made here, although it is no longer on the menu. All one needs to do is ask for it, along with their signature dishes such as Spiedini alla Romana, Clams Oreganeto, and their famous family-style portioned dish called "pasta for four."

Today Giuseppe's grandson, Joseph, who remembers standing on Coca-Cola boxes to reach the counter-tops while learning to cook from his father, Mario, operates the restaurant along with his wife, Barbara, and children, Regina and Michael. But it is his mother, Mama Rose, who, in her nineties, still comes to work every day to make sure that things run the way they were meant to when the restaurant was first opened as Vera Mario's Pizzeria and Restaurant, and of course, to roast her fresh garden-ripened Tuscan peppers for the antipasto.

This classic Neapolitan restaurant, a landmark among landmarks on Arthur Avenue, stands as a testament to "family" and the Italian work ethic that is evident throughout the community.

Above, Giuseppe Migliucci's storefront on Arthur Avenue; interior of Mario's (courtesy of Mario's Restaurant)

Mario's Osso Buco

6 portions veal shank, cut into 2½ to 3-inch pieces
All-purpose flour, for dredging
½ cup extra-virgin olive oil
1 cup finely chopped onion
2 tablespoons chopped lemon peel
1 cup finely chopped carrots
¾ cup finely chopped celery
1 cup dry white wine
3 cups rich chicken stock or broth
Salt and black pepper, to taste

Dredge the meat in flour to coat all sides. Shake off excess. In a heavy casserole or Dutch oven, heat half the oil over medium-high heat. Working in batches so as not to overcrowd the pan, brown the veal on all sides, about 10 minutes per batch. Remove the browned veal shanks with a slotted spoon, add more oil to the pan if necessary, and

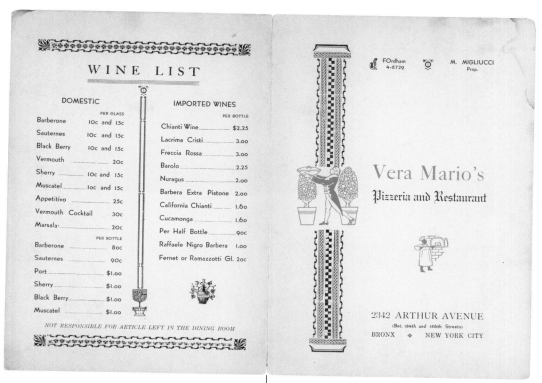

WINE LIST

DOMESTIC

	PER GLASS
Barberone	10c and 15c
Sauternes	10c and 15c
Black Berry	10c and 15c
Vermouth	20c
Sherry	10c and 15c
Muscatel	10c and 15c
Appetitivo	25c
Vermouth Cocktail	30c
Marsala·	20c

	PER BOTTLE
Barberone	80c
Sauternes	90c
Port	$1.00
Sherry	$1.00
Black Berry	$1.00
Muscatel	$1.00

IMPORTED WINES

	PER BOTTLE
Chianti Wine	$2.25
Lacrima Cristi	3.00
Freccia Rossa	3.00
Barolo	2.25
Nuragus	2.00
Barbera Extra Pistone	2.00
California Chianti	1.60
Cucamonga	1.60
Per Half Bottle	90c
Raffaele Nigro Barbera	1.00
Fernet or Ramazzotti Gl.	20c

NOT RESPONSIBLE FOR ARTICLE LEFT IN THE DINING ROOM

FOrdham 4-8729   M. MIGLIUCCI Prop.

Vera Mario's
Pizzeria and Restaurant

2342 ARTHUR AVENUE
(Bet. 184th and 186th Streets)
BRONX ◆ NEW YORK CITY

Menu circa 1940 (courtesy of Mario's Restaurant)

finish browning the remaining veal. Remove and set aside.

Add any reserved oil to the same pan and, over medium heat, slowly sauté the onion, lemon peel, carrots, and celery until tender, about 15 minutes. Stir in the wine, chicken stock, salt, and black pepper. Increase the heat to high and scrape to deglaze pan. Return the browned veal shanks to the pan, cover, and simmer about 1 hour and 15 minutes, until the meat is fork-tender. Carefully remove the meat to a warm platter and heat the sauce over high heat to reduce and thicken it, as desired, about 5 minutes.

Serves 6

Mario's Striped Bass Marechiare

4 fillets striped bass with skin on, about 3 pounds (see note)

All-purpose flour, for dredging

Neutral-flavored oil, for sautéing

12 scrubbed cherrystone clams

12 scrubbed large mussels

2 cups crushed tomatoes, preferably imported Italian

4 cloves garlic, minced

1 tablespoon finely minced fresh parsley

Salt and pepper, to taste

2 tablespoons snipped fresh basil or 1 teaspoon dried

⅓ cup extra-virgin olive oil, preferably light

¾ cup clam juice

1 pound dried spaghetti, boiled in salted water and drained, for serving

Cut the fillets into 8 uniform serving pieces. Dredge in flour and set-aside. In a heavy skillet, pour enough neutral-flavored oil to coat the pan. Heat the oil over medium-high heat. When it is hot, but not smoking, sauté the fish for 1½ to 2 minutes per side, working in batches so as not to overcrowd the pan. Do not overcook the fish. Drain on paper towels.

Arrange the fish in a casserole. Place the clams and mussels around fish. Spoon the tomatoes over all and evenly distribute the garlic, parsley, salt, pepper, and basil evenly. Sprinkle with the olive oil and clam juice. Cover and simmer on top of the stove for about 20 minutes or until the fish flakes easily and shellfish have opened. Discard any shellfish that did not open during cooking. Serve with spaghetti.

Note: Use ½ to ¾ pound per serving. Tile fish may be substituted for striped bass.

Serves 4

Mike's Deli

2344 Arthur Avenue, Bronx

This thriving "deli" has been an institution in the venerable Arthur Avenue Retail Market since 1951. Its story is a true family tale of Italian immigrants — on both sides of the family — coming to America, building their businesses, melding their families, and making a success the "Italian Way."

When Mike's father, Luigi Greco, began making trips from Calabria to the United States in 1895, he never meant to settle permanently in America — his wife, Luisa, was raising their six children and did not want to leave Italy. Luigi traveled between the two countries, living in both and becoming an American citizen though he never "settled" here. In 1947, his seventeen-year-old twin sons, Joe and Mike, immigrated to the United States.

Armed with only $100 each, two suits, strong work ethics, and movie star good looks, Joe and Mike came to seek their fortune. Mike found work in his future father-in-law's grocery store and soon married the boss's only daughter, the talented Antoinetta (Donetta). Before long he felt it was time to make a name for himself, so he opened Mike's Deli in the popular Arthur Avenue Retail Market.

Antoinetta's parents, lovingly called Nonno Gennaro and Nonnabella Capiello Gennaro by the grandchildren, had immigrated to the United States from Naples in 1919. They initially settled in Brooklyn, but soon moved to the Bronx because someone told them that the air was fresher there. (At that time, the area they moved to was a sheep's meadow; later, this same area would become the Arthur Avenue Retail Market). Nonno, a butcher by trade, owned and operated a number of shops with Nonnabella in the Italian section of the Bronx.

Today, with the stewardship of one of Mike's four children, David, the market has grown and expanded, never losing the personal touch that had been so consistent through the many years. At this second-generation American family-owned business, Mike and David are behind the counter every day. A small branch of the deli named the Arthur Avenue Trattoria has opened across the street. At this trattoria, patrons are able to sample all of the dishes that are sold over the counter at the deli. At Mike's Deli you will find fresh mozzarella being stretched into twists and rounds, hear the clamor from the many orders being barked, and, if you are very lucky, you will hear a Puccini aria wafting through the air along with the scent of garlic and oil.

Mike's Deli Caponata

Olive oil, for frying
1 onion, preferably Spanish, cut into ¼-inch dice
1 red bell pepper, stemmed, deseeded, and cut into ¼-inch dice
2 stalks celery, trimmed and cut into ¼-inch dice
1 tablespoon chopped garlic
1 tablespoon capers
8 black olives (pitted)
2 bay leaves
1 firm, large eggplant (about 2 pounds), stemmed and cut into ½-inch cubes
1 quart marinara sauce, preferably Mike's Deli Marinara Sauce
Salt and black pepper, to taste

In a large sauté pan, heat 2 tablespoons of olive oil over high heat. Add the onion and sauté until lightly browned, about 5 minutes. Add the red pepper, celery, garlic, capers, bay leaf, and olives and cook over medium-high heat, for 4 to 5 minutes, stirring occasionally so the flavors mix with one another. Add more oil, if needed, during cooking. Add the eggplant to the pan and cook for 6 to 8 minutes, stirring every minute so the eggplant does not stick to the bottom of the pan. The eggplant is extremely porous and will soak up a lot of oil, so add more oil as needed. When the eggplant begins to soften, add the tomato sauce and stir well to combine. Cook another 8 to 10 minutes, stirring occasionally. Season with salt and pepper. Let cool to room temperature and serve as side dish or relish.

Makes approximately 4 quarts

Mike's Deli Tri Color Salad

2 bunches arugula

1 endive

1 teaspoon fresh-squeezed lemon juice

½ small head radicchio

½ cup extra-virgin olive oil, preferably Mike's "Isabella"

2 tablespoons balsamic vinegar, preferably Mike's "Christian Michael"

2 tablespoons white vinegar

Salt and black pepper, to taste

Trim the root ends off the arugula stems, and wash thoroughly under cold water. Drain well and set aside. Cut the root end off the endive and cut crosswise into ¼-inch rounds. Place in a bowl with water to cover and the lemon juice. Remove any bad leaves from the radicchio and cut in two lengthwise, right through the stem end. Wash, if any grain or dirt is visible. Set the radicchio on a cutting board, flat-side down, and slice crosswise into strips (chiffonade). Drain the endive.

In a large mixing bowl, toss the arugula, endive, and radicchio with the oil and vinegar. Season with salt and pepper.

Mama Greco's Italian Cheesecake from the Arthur Avenue Café

1 (48-ounce) container ricotta cheese

2 cups sugar

8 large eggs, yolks and whites separated

½ cup sifted all-purpose flour

Grated rind of 1 lemon

1 teaspoon pure vanilla extract

4 ounces cream cheese (½ cup), softened

Butter to grease pan

½ cup graham cracker crumbs

Mike Greco, circa 1962 (courtesy of Mike's Deli)

Preheat the oven to 425°F.

Drain the ricotta cheese in a cheese cloth–lined colander or fine-meshed seive to extract the excess moisture. The longer you drain (up to an hour), the more moisture you extract and the creamier your cheesecake will taste.

In a large bowl, beat the drained ricotta cheese until smooth with an electric mixer on medium-high speed. Gradually add 1½ cups of the sugar and the egg yolks, one at a time, beating after each addition. Beat in the flour, lemon rind, and vanilla.

In a separate bowl, beat the egg whites with the remaining ½ cup of sugar until stiff. Add the cream cheese and beat until blended. Gently fold the cream cheese mixture into the ricotta mixture.

Line the bottom of a 12-inch springform pan with wax paper, parchment, or tin foil. Grease the pan liner with butter and evenly distribute the graham cracker crumbs across the bottom of the pan. Pour the batter into the prepared pan. Bake for 10 minutes, and then lower the temperature to 350°F and bake for 1 hour more, until the top of the cheesecake is golden-brown. Turn off the oven and allow to cool in the oven with door closed.

"The meal is remembered long after the kiss has been forgotten."
Italian proverb

Bensonhurst, Brooklyn

Sunday morning just isn't the same in Bensonhurst anymore. The now quiet streets, absent of honking cars, kids playing, and people yelling to their neighbors, doesn't have the same ambience. And long gone is the warm scent of tomato sauce wafting from the windows of every home. Times have changed for the most treasured of Italian communities. What used to be a loud, friendly, gaudy Italian American enclave has all but disappeared.

Yet, the memories of those who lived there will never fade. The holidays and the celebrations have moved on to Staten Island, New Jersey, or Long Island, making the massive family dinners of the old neighborhood in Bensonhurst just a recollection in the mind's eye.

Originally settled by the Dutch in 1661 as part of the town of New Utrecht, Bensonhurst today is bordered by 61st Street, McDonald and Stillwell Avenues, Gravesend Bay, 14th Avenue, and 86th Street, and includes the areas known as Mapleton and New Utrecht. In the late 1880s, the Benson Farm was parceled into 20 x 100-foot lots, thus establishing the suburb of Bensonhurst.

The 1890s brought wealthy landowners to Bensonhurst, who built summer homes and marinas among the farms and woodlands. It was hoped that the Bath Beach-Coney

The Feast of San Gennaro, New York City (courtesy of Manhattan Post Card Co.)

Island railroad, built along the shore, would enhance the community of "Bensonhurst by the Sea," largely due to the success of the Coney Island amusement park, but tourism efforts were unsuccessful. The arrival of the Fourth Avenue subway line in 1915 made the area accessible to New Yorkers and many successful immigrants fled the Lower East Side of Manhattan to build homes in Bensonhurst.

The construction of high-rise apartment buildings in the 1930s along with single-family and attached houses made Bensonhurst a haven for middle-class families with strong ethnic roots. It was common to find two or three generations all living on the same block if not in the same two-family home.

According to some historians, Bensonhurst remains the most authentic Little Italy in New York. Its main street, 86th Street between 14th Avenue and Stillwell Avenue, is the commercial spine of the neighborhood. Eighteenth Avenue is lined with countless family-owned cafés, bakeries, food shops, pork and pasta stores, and restaurants decorated in the colors of green, red, and white. The fruit stands still remain, but the tradition of *abbanniata* (loudly hawking your merchandise) is forever gone.

At one time, Bensonhurst was a classic Italian neighborhood, a place of tidy two-family brick homes adorned with Madonnas and American flags. This community contributed heavily to the entertainment industry, producing countless actors, comedians, and musicians and by being the setting for movies or television shows — *The Honeymooners, Welcome Back Kotter,* and *Saturday Night Fever,* to name a few. And the neighborhood has had a strong influence on the New York City dialect, as well as its gestures, food, and music. The Italians, who gave the city so much of its energy and charm, have declined in numbers here. What we are left with are the memories of a

different time that, for some, evoke the '70s when young Italians taught the rest of us how to disco and how to strut!

Despite the fact that immigrant groups want to continue their allegiance to the old neighborhoods, the children of these middle-class working families are often professionals and business people who desire a suburban environment with larger homes and less concrete.

On 18th Avenue, the site of the annual Feast of Santa Rosalia, men still sip espresso in cafés, but there are fewer men and fewer cafés. Chinese novelty stores and beauty parlors are now replacing the cafés as the inevitable stream of new immigrants arrives, bringing change with them.

L & B Spumoni Gardens

2725 86th Street, Brooklyn

The neighborhood might be changing, but don't tell that to one of the four generations of Barbati family members who have been running L & B Spumoni Gardens since 1939. While many Italians are losing their "comfort zone" in the neighborhood, and moving up, so to speak, other nationalities move in to take their place. This, however, does not have any effect on the popularity of this Brooklyn landmark.

Ludovico Barbati arrived at Ellis Island in 1917 from Torella Di Lombardi and one year later met his wife, Paolina Maugeri, with whom he would have six children.

Through hard work, Ludovico was eventually able to establish himself as the premier spumoni maker in Bensonhurst. Learning his trade from a baker in the neighborhood, he began to make spumoni and ices in a garage on West 8th Street in Brooklyn and peddled them by way of a horse-drawn wagon. (The horse was lovingly called "Babe.")

As he became more succesful, he employed the skills of his friends from "the Old Country" — carpenters, brick layers, and cement workers — to help build what would eventually become the site of L & B Spumoni Gardens today.

Still popular and still busy, they now serve a full menu, including their famous thick Sicilian pies, and you can be assured that you will always be greeted by a family member. Just order your "square slice," and the vanilla, chocolate, and pistachio spumoni in a paper cup, take a seat at one of the picnic tables on a sunny day, and hope for a glimpse of the many celebrities who never miss an opportunity to stop by for a slice.

Ludorico Barbati, his spumoni cart, and his horse, Babe (courtesy of L & B Spumoni Gardens)

(courtesy of L & B Spumoni Gardens)

L & B Spumoni Gardens Shrimp in Lobster Sauce (Toramina)

5 large shrimp, peeled, cleaned, and split

¼ cup all-purpose flour seasoned with salt and pepper, plus 1 teaspoon for thickening stock

4 large eggs, beaten

½ cup extra-virgin olive oil, preferably Decco

¼ cup seafood stock (recipe follows) or equal parts bottled clam juice and water or clam juice and vegetable stock, at room temperature

1 small clove garlic

2 (2-ounce) cooked lobster tails, peeled and cut into 6 pieces

3 baby portobello mushrooms, sliced

1 tablespoon butter

¼ cup Marsala wine

¼ cup sweet Italian vermouth

Salt and pepper, to taste

1 teaspoon coarsely chopped fresh Italian (flat-leaf) parsley

Dredge the shrimp in the seasoned flour and then in the egg wash.

In a large, deep skillet, heat the oil over high heat. When the oil is hot (about 275°F), shallow-fry the shrimp until golden brown. (**Note:** If you don't have a deep-fat or candy thermometer, you may test the heat of the oil by dropping a small drop of egg wash batter in the oil. When it comes to top and is browned, the oil is ready.) Remove the shrimp with a slotted spoon and place on paper towels to drain. Drain the skillet of most of the oil, leaving just enough to thinly coat the bottom of the pan, and set aside.

In a sauté pan, warm the stock over very low heat. Slowly whisk in 1 teaspoon of flour until it is completely blended. Keep warm over very low heat.

Set the skillet with the reserved oil over medium heat. Add the garlic, lobster, and mushrooms and sauté for 2 minutes. Add the butter, wine, vermouth, salt and pepper and bring to a boil over medium heat. Add the seafood stock and simmer over low heat, stirring occasionally. As the sauce starts to thicken, add the parsley and serve immediately with cooked pasta of your choice.

Serves 2

Seafood Stock

2 small whole white onions, coarsely chopped

2 whole cloves garlic, coarsely chopped

2 teaspoons extra-virgin olive oil

3 gallons water

1 celery stalk, coarsely chopped

6 to 8 hard-shelled clams, well rinsed

6 to 8 mussels, cleaned (see tip)

Shells from 16 shrimp

Skeleton of 1 lobster

6 sea scallops (see note)

Salt and pepper to taste

In a large stockpot, sauté the onions and garlic in the olive oil over medium heat. Add the water, celery, clams, and mussels, and let cook, covered, for about 5 minutes. Remove and discard any unopened mussels or clams. Add the shrimp shells, lobster skeleton, and scallops and let simmer for 1 hour. Season with salt and pepper. Strain and use as directed. Will keep in the freezer for 6 months.

Note: Do not remove the little piece of fiber that attaches to the scallop to its shell as it is very flavorful.

Makes about 3 gallons

Tip: Cleaning Mussels

Discard any chipped or broken mussels. If you have time, place the mussels in a bowl with cold water for about 20 minutes. This will help the mussels to release silt. Carefully remove the mussels from the bowl, leaving the silt in the bottom of the bowl. Rinse the mussels, debeard them, and rinse again. (To debeard a mussel, pull off the small amount of threadlike vegetative growth along the flat side of the mussel.)

Rudy Giuliani with L & B staff (courtesy of L & B Spumoni Gardens)

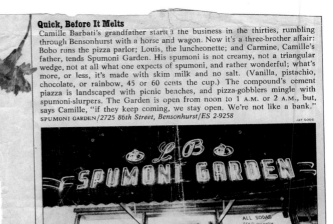

(courtesy of L & B Spumoni Gardens)

Sardinian-Style Tomato and Fresh Orange Sauce with Roasted Zucchini

Extra-virgin olive oil, preferably Decco®

1 clove garlic, left whole or thinly sliced

Juice of 4 to 6 oranges

4 cups vegetable or chicken stock

4 small zucchini, preferably Italian, cut in ½-inch dice

1 pound dried mezzi rigatoni

16 fresh basil leaves

8 canned plum tomatoes, cut in half (from one 14.5-ounce can)

1 tablespoon grated orange zest

1 sprig Italian (flat-leaf) parsley

Salt and black pepper, to taste

Preheat the oven to 400°F.

Pour just enough oil to coat the bottom of a 12-inch sauté pan and set over medium-high heat. Add the garlic and sauté until lightly browned, about 2 to 3 minutes. Add the orange juice and vegetable stock and simmer on low heat until thick, about 10 minutes.

Bring a generously salted, 6-quart stock pot of water to a boil on medium heat. While the water is coming to a boil, pan-roast the zucchini. Toss the zucchini with enough olive oil to coat (about 4 tablespoons), salt and pepper in a baking dish and roast in the oven for 30 minutes.

When the vegetable stock mixture is thickened and the zucchini is done, add the rigatoni to the boiling water. Cook until al dente, about 8 minutes. Drain well.

Add the basil, canned tomatoes, orange zest, and parsley to the thickened vegetable stock. Stir to combine and heat through over medium heat. Add salt and pepper and the cooked pasta. Toss the pasta until well coated with the sauce and serve.

Serves 4

A baker's hands (courtesy of DiCamillo Baking Co.)

"Hunger makes hard beans sweet."
Italian proverb

Boston, Massachusetts's North End

The true heartbeat of the city of Boston is in the historic Italian North
End, where history, cappuccino, wine, pizza, pasta, authentic architecture, and lively street life makes you feel as if you are in Italy. Just north of Boston's hub, on a hillside rising from the historic Boston harbor, is where the burgeoning population from Italy made its home.

The Italian masses that arrived in the North End of the Boston Harbor area found a rundown, overcrowded slum with deteriorating tenements and a general distain for foreigners. The first wave of Italian immigrants, numbering only about 200, came in the 1860s from Genoa and settled in a three-block area off Fulton Street. Here they made their living as fruit and vegetable vendors and as peddlers of wine, cheese, and olive oil. During the 1880s the Irish immigrants, who first populated the area, began to relocate to other neighborhoods. Following the Genoese, came the Campanians, and then the Sicilians who, by 1925, had colonized the wharf area along the harbor and took part in the very profitable commercial fishing fleets. The Avellinese, the Neopolitans, and the Abruzzesians soon landed and they found work in the construction trades as masons, metalworkers, carpenters, and laborers. Each group settled within its own area in the greater North End. By 1900, the Italian population of

the North End was 14,000 and it would double in the next 20 years. By 1930, there were 44,000 Italians packed into an area of less than one square mile.

Over the decades, as Protestant churches were acquired by the Catholic Archdiocese of Boston they became places of worship for the Italian Americans who now lived there. In 1899, St. Leonard's Church was founded, making it the first Italian church in New England and the second oldest in America. Around the same time, settlement houses became popular to assist newly arrived immigrants in adjusting to their new lives in America. They provided food and aid and developed the city's first public children's playground.

Most Italians found life hard, both economically and socially, in the North End. The rise of Bolshevism and the growth of Italian Fascism created a hostile political climate toward immigrants. But even in the midst of hardships and challenges, there were great success stories. It was in the North End that the Prince Pasta Company was founded by three Sicilian friends, Gaetano LaMarco, Giuseppe Seminara, and Michele Cantella. Another prominent business was founded by Luigi Pastene, who emigrated from Italy in 1848 and began by selling produce with a pushcart. By 1870, he was joined by his son who helped him establish Pastene as a specialty and Italian import grocer. Today, the Pastene Corporation has distribution in the United States as well as in Italy.

It is said that the families of the North End had the same basic menu scheduled for each day of the week. Sunday would be tomato sauce (called "tomato gravy") with any variety of meats or chicken, Monday was soup day using the bones of the meats or chicken consumed on Sunday, Tuesday and Thursday were the leftovers from the other days and Wednesday was a variety of choices, and because, of course, no meat could be eaten on Friday, that was the night fish was served. It was stuffed, baked, fried, or

steamed and served with all sorts of vegetables and many kinds of pastas and potatoes. Saturday was generally a treat as it was an "anything goes" day. Everyone ate well, even though times were tough.

The North End has had its share of national incidents. The Great Molasses Flood of 1919 took 21 lives and caused widespread destruction when a 50-foot tank filled with 2.3 million gallons of molasses exploded on the North End waterfront. And a little over a year later, two North Enders, Nicola Sacco and Bartolomeo Vanzetti, were arrested and accused of robbing and murdering a paymaster and his guard from a local shoe company. The witnesses said that the men "looked Italian" and since Sacco and Vanzetti had fled to Mexico to avoid serving in World War I, which the United States was engaged in, they were considered suspect. Even though the two of them had solid alibis, their radical beliefs were emphasized, as was the fact that their alibis were corroborated by other Italians. They were found guilty and sentenced to death. Despite the public outcry, demonstrations, and appeals across the United States and Europe, they were executed on August 23, 1927, an event attended by several thousand spectators. The funeral procession was the largest in Boston's history, attracting more than 7,000 marchers. More than 200,000 people crowded the streets to watch it.

The North End had to contend with an unsavory criminal reputation as it was rife with sailors, gamblers, and brothels. The most prolific criminal was one of their own, Charles A. Ponzi, who became one of the greatest "confidence men" of modern times. He perpetrated a crime — the "Ponzi scheme" — on his own people by offering to pay a 50 percent premium on an investment. The scheme was based on Ponzi purchasing coupons, known as International Rely Coupons, and redeeming them. Word spread, money began to pour in, and by 1920, he had promissory notes valued at 15 million

S. ANTONIO
DA PADOVA DI MONTEFALCHONE

7up

(courtesy of Caffé Vittoria)

dollars. The bubble burst in 1920 when it was found that he had never bought the coupons and that investors were being paid with the money brought into the scheme by subsequent investors — not from real profits.

By the end of WWII, the past prejudice against Italian Americans began to diminish and a new political face began to surface as many of the locals ran for political office. In many ways, they helped to improve the living conditions in the North End.

Today, while Italian Americans still comprise almost 40 percent of the resident population, many urban, upscale professionals have moved into this historic and thriving neighborhood. Despite the fact that at one time there were fifty individual religious societies and only twelve remain today, these societies, with their feasts and processions, remain an integral part of the life and culture of the area. The first annual Fisherman's Feast was held in the North End in 1911, when the fishermen from Sicily brought their sixteenth-century traditional feast to the Unites States. The feast is an event of epic proportions: The Madonna del Soccorso is paraded through the streets, those who founded the feast are remembered with a blessing of the waters, and everyone enjoys plates of sausages, calamari, and pasta. Though times have changed in Boston's North End, one can still walk along the curved streets, smell the garlic and olive oil, sip an espresso, and breathe the scent of the nearby sea.

Cantina Italiana

346 Hanover Street, Boston

There are a lot of reasons to visit the North End, Boston's Little Italy, but if you come for nothing else but the bombolotti, it will be worth trip. It is what made Cantina Italiana famous. This wagon wheel-shaped tube of pasta, which looks like a rigatoni with spokes, is homemade here and is the dish of choice. The die that's used to form and cut the dough was patented and developed here for Cantina Italiana and its sister restaurant, Ristorante Fiore, also in the North End. They are the only restaurants to serve this unique pasta.

Cantina Italiana boasts that it is the oldest restaurant in the North End. Since its opening in 1931, the restaurant has seen only two owners. Its current owner, Fiore Colella, was born in 1958 in Avellino, in Southern Italy. He knew that his interests went well beyond his small-town borders. Late in immigrating to the United States, Fiore left his village to fulfill his desire for a better life. Working as a dishwasher at twelve years old, in the very restaurant he would one day own, he began to learn English and the skills that would enable him to succeed. From dishwasher, he became the pizza chef and, with determination and hard work, within ten years he learned the cooking skills necessary to run the little restaurant. Since 1980, Fiore Colella has been the owner of Cantina Italiana and has made it into one of the most recognizable landmarks on Hanover Street.

The original neon sign in front of Cantina Italiana is a neon sign lover's find. A huge bottle of red wine tips on its side and drops of the wine appear to spill down into a wine glass. You could watch this sign for hours while enjoying some of the best pasta on Hanover Street.

(courtesy of Cantina Italiana)

Cantina Italiana Spaghetti Alle Vongole

4 tablespoons extra-virgin olive oil, plus extra for drizzling

4 cloves garlic, chopped

14 baby hard-shelled clams, such as littlenecks, well rinsed

1 cup bottled clam juice

4 tablespoons dry white wine

8 ounces dried spaghetti

Chopped fresh parsley, for garnish

Bring 3 quarts of generously salted water to a boil.

While the water is coming to a boil, heat the oil in a sauté pan with a tightly-fitting lid over medium heat. Add the garlic and sauté until it turns slightly brown. Add the clams, clam juice, and white wine. Cover and continue to cook until the clams open, about 5 minutes. Periodically check the clams; as soon as they open, remove the pan from the heat but leave covered. Discard any clams that did not open.

While the clams are cooking, add the spaghetti to the boiling water. Cook until al dente, about 10 minutes. Drain the spaghetti well and add it to the pan with the clams. Toss together and transfer to two plates or bowls. Sprinkle with parsley and drizzle on some olive oil.

Serves 2

Cantina Italiana Bombolotti Buongustaia

4 tablespoons extra-virgin olive oil

1 onion, diced

½ pound hot Italian sausage links, sliced

1 (14.5-ounce) can ounces canned whole, peeled Italian Roma tomatoes, chopped

6 fresh basil leaves, chopped

Salt and black pepper, to taste

12 ounces dried rigatoni pasta (see note)

4 ounces Parmigiano-Reggiano cheese, grated

4 ounces Pecorino cheese, shaved

4 ounces goat cheese, diced

In a large pot, bring 2 quarts of water to a boil with a couple pinches of salt. Preheat the oven to 450°F.

In a large frying or sauté pan, heat the oil over high heat. Add the onions and sausage and sauté until golden brown. Add the tomatoes, basil, and a pinch each of salt and pepper, reduce heat to medium and cook for 10 minutes.

When the water comes to a boil, add the pasta and cook until al dente, about 10 minutes. Drain the pasta well and add to the pan with the sauce. Add the Parmigiano-Reggiano and the Pecorino cheeses and toss. Transfer to an oven-safe baking dish and top with the goat cheese. Bake until golden brown and serve.

Note: At Cantina Italiana, the famed bombolotti pasta is used to make Bombolotti Buongustaia and Bombolotti Del Marinaio. Unfortunately, for those not living in the Boston area, bombolotti pasta can only be enjoyed at its source, at the Cantina Italiana restaurant. Rigatoni, however, makes an excellent substitute for both dishes.

Serves 2

Cantina Italiana Bombolotti Del Marinaio

4 tablespoons extra-virgin olive oil

2 cloves garlic, chopped

8 ounces fresh lobster tail

4 ounces fresh lobster meat

1 (14.5-ounce) can whole, peeled Italian Roma tomatoes

6 fresh basil leaves, chopped

Salt and black pepper, to taste

12 ounces dried rigatoni pasta (see note)

In a large pot, bring 3 quarts of water to a boil with a couple pinches of salt.

In a large frying pan, heat the oil over medium heat. Add the garlic and sauté until golden brown. Add the lobster tail and lobster meat and cook, uncovered, stirring occasionally, for 3 minutes. Add the tomatoes, basil and a pinch each of salt and pepper. Stir to combine and cook for 10 minutes over medium heat, or until the lobster meat becomes white and opaque.

When water comes to a boil, add the pasta and cook until al dente, about 10 minutes. Drain well and toss in the sauce and serve.

Serves 2

Bijou Theatre and Church Street,
New Haven, Conn.

216460

Vintage postcard of Bijou Theatre and Church Street, New Haven, C.T. (courtesy of Frank Rully)

Frank Pepe Pizzeria

157 Wooster Street, New Haven

There are allegedly 300 coal-burning ovens left on the East Coast. If you want a pizza that is spectacular in every way, you want it cooked in a coal-burning oven. It's illegal now to burn coal for heating in some cities, but if a coal-burning oven already exists in a restaurant, its use is grandfathered in, but only for cooking purposes. The oven temperatures reach 600 degrees with the coals themselves reaching close to 2000 degrees. It takes three days for the oven to heat up and three days to cool, so needless to say, the oven stays lit.

In 1909, seventeen-year-old Frank Pepe arrived in the United States from a small town south of Naples and, after a stint of selling locks and keys, he returned to Italy to fight in WWI. When he returned, he apprenticed as a baker and devised new ways to make pizza, using leftovers from the previous day. (Clams served on the half-shell one day, made an excellent pizza topping the next day.) Following this invention, Frank made it his specialty to develop alternative toppings for the flat breads that he was baking.

In 1925, Frank opened Frank Pepe Pizzeria Napoletana on Wooster Street in the heart of New Haven's Little Italy. Frank and his wife, Filomena, lived above the pizzeria and raised their two daughters, Serafina and Elizabeth, there. This

Commercial portrait, circa 1935, with backdrop of Amalfi Coast (courtesy of Francis Roselli)

Frank and wife Filomena at new location, 157 Wooster Street, circa 1940 (courtesy of Francis Roselli)

venture was not only a means to feed his family, but a way to employ and feed his vast number of friends and relatives.

Serafina's son, Gary Bimonte, and his cousin, Francis Rosselli, began working at the pizzeria in 1975 and, with six other relatives, they remain there today, making their most-famous and most-ordered pizza, the white clam pie. This over-the-top pizza, made with fresh shucked clams, Parmigiano-Reggiano cheese, garlic, oregano, and olive oil, is a legend and one of the most popular pizzas in the United States.

Frank Pepe viewed pizza as "the poor man's answer to hunger." But at this little slice of pizza heaven, these fabulous pizzas do more than fill an empty belly — they delight and nourish the soul!

Frank Pepe's White Clam Pizza

Frank Pepe's doesn't measure when making this divine pizza, but, these few guidelines may help.

10 to 12 ounces pizza dough of your choice

3 tablespoons extra-virgin olive oil

3 large cloves garlic, chopped

1 dozen freshly shucked clams, coarsely chopped (reserve any juice)

1 teaspoon dried oregano

2 tablespoons grated Parmesan cheese

Preheat the oven to 400°F.

Place the dough in the center of a pizza stone or a 9 x 12-inch sheet pan. Flatten and stretch the dough by hand to about 10 inches in diameter on the stone or to the edges of the sheet pan.

Brush the olive oil on the dough. Sprinkle the chopped garlic all over the dough, and then spread the clams around the pie with a dash of their own juice. Sprinkle with the oregano and cheese. Bake until the pie is charred on the edges, about 15 minutes.

Makes 1 round (10-inch) pizza or 1 rectangular 9 x 12-inch pizza

The famous White Clam Pizza (courtesy of Frank Pepe Pizzeria)

Original location at 157 Wooster Street, circa 1930 (courtesy of Francis Roselli)

Consiglio's Restaurant

165 Wooster Street, New Haven

When Salvatore and Annunziata (Nancy) Consiglio emigrated in 1912 from the Amalfi Coast to the United States, they arrived with the second wave of Italian immigration. The family settled in the area in New Haven known as Wooster Square, home to many of the immigrants from the Amalfi Coast of Italy. Members of the Consiglio family apprenticed in many restaurants until, in 1938, with the help of all seven children, they were able to open a small family restaurant called The Big Apple. Their restaurant was nothing more than an extension of their own kitchen as they made everything from scratch and catered mostly to family and friends. Laborers and local dock workers from Long Wharf flocked there for the food and to rekindle their memories of Amalfi.

Urban renewal threatened to come to New Haven in the 1960s and to cut a swath across the square, which would have forced many business owners and residents to relocate. Anticipating the destruction of their original location, the Big Apple moved across the street to its present location, a former pastry shop, and was renamed Consiglio's. Fortunately for the community, the square was saved. After the move, one of the Consiglio's sons, Pat, and his wife, Barbara, ran the business. Today, it is still a family affair with their daughters, Trish and Laura, running the business; Aunt Maria Apicella, who has worked there since she was eight years old, making the cavatelli; and Aunt Annie Abbenate, at eighty-eight years old, serving as the restaurant's hostess. The fourth generation is already in place to take over.

Gary Trudeau of *Doonesbury* fame dined at Consiglio's while at Yale, as did the late Senator Edward Kennedy and numerous politicians, sports figures, and film stars, but the Consiglios make no distinctions — everyone is treated like family. With its cozy ambience and excellent food, it's no wonder that customers keep returning to this quintessential Italian restaurant.

Menu cover from Consiglio's (courtesy of Consiglio's)

Consiglio's Cavatelli Pasta with Pesto

Fresh Cavatelli Pasta

(Makes 20 to 22 8-ounce portions)

6 eggs

1 (48-ounce) container ricotta cheese

8 cups all-purpose flour

1 tablespoon salt

1 teaspoon black pepper

¼ cup vegetable oil

Pesto Sauce

2 cups packed fresh basil leaves

½ cup packed fresh Italian (flat-leaf) parsley leaves

2 cloves garlic

¼ cup pignoli nuts (pine nuts)

½ cup extra-virgin olive oil

¼ cup grated Parmesan cheese

To make the pesto: Place the ingredients for the pesto in a blender or food processor and blend until smooth.

To make the pasta: Using a stand mixer with a dough hook, mix together the ingredients for the pasta for 2 minutes, until the dough holds together firmly and can be cut into sections with a knife.

Roll the dough into long "snakes" about ½-inch in diameter. Cut the snakes into 1-inch-long sections and roll a pastry cutter across the top to create a design.

Divide the cavatelli into 8-ounce portions. You should have about 20 to 22 portions. Set aside two 8-ounce portions for now and freeze the remainder. Cavatelli can be frozen for 3 months. Take out the desired portions as needed.

Bring a large pot of salted water to rolling boil. Add the 16 ounces of fresh cavatelli. When they float to the top, they are done. Drain and toss with the pesto sauce.

Note: Making fresh cavatelli is an undertaking, but one worth doing. At Consiglio's, they like to make a large batch of cavatelli of twenty to twenty-two eight ounce portions. It freezes wonderfully, which makes the effort worthwhile.

Serves 2

Consiglio's Christmas Soup

2 tablespoons butter

1 large onion, diced

2 (28-ounce) cans whole, peeled Italian plum tomatoes, with their juice

1½ cups canned chicken broth

½ cup heavy cream

1 pinch dried oregano

1 pinch of dried basil

1 pinch of dried parsley

½ teaspoon celery seed

Salt and black pepper, to taste

¾ cup grated Gouda cheese

Chopped fresh Italian (flat-leaf) parsley, for garnish

Melt the butter in a heavy saucepan over medium heat. Add the onion and sauté about 8 minutes. Add tomatoes with juices and chicken broth. Break up the tomatoes with a wooden spoon and simmer for 30 minutes. Add the cream, herbs, celery seed and continue to simmer 15 minutes. Season with salt and pepper and ladle soup into 4 bowls. Sprinkle with the grated Gouda cheese and chopped parsley.

Serves 4

BRACIOLA DI MANZO
Beef roll, seasoned with chopped parsley, garlic, grated cheese, salt, pepper, and cooked in tomato sauce.
Vegetable or Spaghetti

EGGPLANT PARMIGIANA
Melted layer of mozzarella cheese between slices of sauteed eggplant, topped with tomato sauce.
Vegetable or Spaghetti

SALTIMBOCCA A ROMANA
Veal rolls stuffed with thin slices of Italian ham, mozzarella cheese, sauteed in butter and wine sauce, and smothered with mushrooms. Served over Green Noodles.
Vegetable

SHRIMP MARINARA
Jumbo Shrimps simmered in spicy marinara sauce, and served over spaghetti.

Children Menu
FRUIT CUP
SOUP
CHOICE OF
SPAGHETTI
ZITI MACARONI
OR
RAVIOLI
WITH TOMATO SAUCE
ICE CREAM
SODA
OR
MILK

A La Carte

APPETIZERS
FRESH FRUIT COCKTAIL AU SHERBET . . . .   FRESH JUMBO SHRIMP COCKTAIL. .
TOSSED SALAD . . . .   FETTUCCINI ALFREDO . . . .
STUFFED ESCAROLE . . . .   FRIED SQUIDS . . . .
BROCCOLI WITH LEMON . . . .   FRIED MOZZARELLA . . . .
BAKED STUFFED CLAMS . . . .   SCUNGILLI SALAD . . . .
CHERRYSTONE CLAMS (6) . . . .   ZUPPA DI CLAMS (RED OR WHITE SA
ASSORTED ANTIPASTO . . . .

FARINACEOUS
SPAGHETTI, BUTTER AND CHEESE . . . .   BAKED CANNELLONI . . . .
ZITI MACARONI WITH TOMATO SAUCE . . . .   HOME-MADE FETTUCCINI . . . .
SPAGHETTI, MARINARA SAUCE . . . .   LASAGNE IMBOTTITE . . . .
SPAGHETTI, OIL AND GARLIC . . . .   CAVATELLI . . . .
SPAGHETTI, MEAT BALLS . . . .   SPAGHETTI, CALAMARI (SQUID) . .
SPAGHETTI, OIL AND ANCHOVIES . . . .   SPAGHETTI, WHITE CLAM SAUCE . .
SPAGHETTI, ITALIAN SAUSAGE . . . .   BAKED ZITI IN CASSEROLE . . .
MANICOTTI (CHEESE FILLING) . . . .   STEAMED CLAMS OVER SPAGHETTI
RAVIOLI (MEAT OR CHEESE FILLING) . . . .   SPAGHETTI, WITH MEAT BALL
(CHILD'S PORTION)

VEAL SPECIALTIES
VEAL CUTLET PARMIGIANA . . . .
VEAL FLORENTINE . . . .
VEAL MARSALA . . . .
SALTIMBOCCA A ROMANA WITH MUSHROOMS . . . .
CHOICE OF SPAGHETTI OR VEGETABLE SERVED WITH VEAL PLATTERS

SEAFOOD IN SEASON
CALAMARI (SQUID) . . . .   SHRIMP A MARINARA . . . .
DEEP SEA SCALLOPS . . . .   SHRIMP SCAMPI . . . .
COMBINATION SEAFOOD PLATTER . . . .   LOBSTER FRA DIAVOLO . . . .
FRESH FRIED JUMBO SHRIMP . . . .   BROILED LOBSTER (SHRIMP FILLIN
ALL SEAFOOD PLATTERS SERVED WITH SPAGHETTI OR VEGETABLE

STEAKS AND CHOPS
BRACIOLA DI MANZO . . . .
BROILED PORK CHOPS WITH PEPPERS . . . .
BROILED DEL MONICO STEAK, MUSHROOMS . . . .
DEL MONICO STEAK A PIZZAIOLA . . . .

POULTRY
HALF BROILED SPRING CHICKEN . . . .
BONELESS CHICKEN PARMIGIANA . . . .
HALF SPRING CHICKEN A CACCIATORA (WITH MUSHROOMS) . . . .
CHOICE OF SPAGHETTI OR VEGETABLE SERVED WITH STEAKS, CHOPS AND POULT

DESSERTS
SPUMONI . . . .   TORTONI . . . .   RICOTTA PIE . . .
ICE CREAM. . . . .   GELATI . . . .   DEMI TASSE . . .
SHERBET . . . .   RUM CAKE . . . .   ITALIAN PASTRIE

GARLIC BREAD FOR (2) . . . .

Menu from Consiglio's (courtesy of Consiglio's)

©2008. J.R. Muratore

Venda Ravioli

265 Atwells Avenue, Providence

When Mary and David Venteroni first established Venda in the Italian section of Providence, Rhode Island in 1938, they could never have imagined how their little shop would grow. Their place was so small that there was hardly room for customers. Working out of a cramped 200-square-foot shop with only fourteen feet of counter space, they kept their inventory small, selling only homemade cheese ravioli, egg noodles, and cavatelli. Since 1972, when Alan Costantino purchased Venda from the Venteronis, it has become a local and national destination.

Costantino's venture into the business of food purely by accident — when he was looking for property to purchase. Venda was for sale and with no experience in the food business, he took a chance. The business blossomed from a small mom-and-pop store with a mere three products to a food emporium *extraordinaire*!

In 2001, Venda moved to 265 Atwells Avenue and quadrupled in size. Venda now has over 200 different varieties of pasta, a cold-cut meat counter, an enormous gourmet shop, an international cheese counter, freshly baked breads, a butcher counter, and aisles of Italian products ranging from cookies and coffee to polenta and pots and pans. They even have a certified olive oil consultant on the premises. There is an espresso bar, a gelato bar, and an Italian café. Outside is the most delightful piazza, the DiPasquale Plaza, with table service rivaling anything you would find in Rome. The sounds of Frank Sinatra, opera, concerts, and doo-wop music fill the air and the heady scent of linguini with pesto sauce is overwhelming. If there ever was a direct line to Italy, this local treasure would be it.

(courtesy of Venda Ravioli)

Venda's Baccalà Con Olive Verdi (Fried Salt Cod with Green Olives)

1 pound center-cut salt cod (baccalà), cut into 2-inch pieces
2 medium onions, coarsely chopped
⅓ cup extra-virgin olive oil
All-purpose flour, for dredging
2 tablespoons minced fresh Italian (flat-leafed) parsley
⅔ cup Sicilian green olives, pitted and cut into slivers
Lemon wedges, for serving

In a large bowl of cold water, let the cod soak, chilled, changing the water at least 12 times, for 2 days.

Drain the cod and pat it dry between paper towels. In a heavy, nonstick skillet, cook the onions in the oil over medium heat until softened and transfer them with a slotted spoon to a bowl, letting as much of the oil as possible drain back into the skillet.

Dredge the cod in flour, knocking off the excess. Heat the oil remaining in the skillet over moderately high heat until it is hot but not smoking, and sauté the cod in 2 batches, turning it once, until it is golden. Add the onions, parsley, and olives. Cook the mixture over moderately low heat, turning the cod once or twice, for 10 minutes, or until the cod just flakes. Serve the cod warm or at room temperature with the lemon wedges.

Serves 2

Venda's Tiramisu

2 egg yolks

2 tablespoons sugar

2 teaspoons pure vanilla extract

1 pound mascarpone cheese

¾ cup strong black coffee

1 tablespoon Kahlua® or other coffee liqueur

24 small savoiardi (lady fingers)

1 to 2 tablespoons unsweetened cocoa powder

In large bowl, mix together the egg yolks, sugar, and vanilla with an electric mixer on slow speed until the consistency is creamy. Gently fold in the mascarpone to make a cream.

In a small bowl, mix together the coffee and coffee liqueur. Dip the savoiardi for a second or two into the coffee mixture, making sure they do not become too soggy.

On individual serving plates, starting with the savoiardi, arrange alternating layers of savoiardi and mascarpone cream, ending with the cream.

Dust the servings generously with the cocoa powder, and refrigerate for 1 to 2 hours to set and chill before serving.

Venda's Bolognese Sauce

¼ cup extra-virgin olive oil

2 ounces (½ stick) butter

2 ounces salt pork, diced

1 large onion, diced

½ pound Italian sweet sausage meat, casings removed

½ pound lean ground beef

4 chicken livers, finely chopped

2 cloves garlic, minced

½ teaspoon rosemary

1 bay leaf

¼ teaspoon freshly ground black pepper

¼ cup dry white wine

1 cup canned whole, peeled plum tomatoes

2 medium-size ripe tomatoes, finely chopped

Pinch of freshly grated nutmeg

1 cup boiling hot water

In a large saucepan over medium heat, combine the olive

The outdoor garden at Venda Ravioli (courtesy of Venda Ravioli)

oil, butter, and salt pork. Add the onions and brown slowly over medium heat. Add the sausage, ground beef, and chopped chicken livers. Brown slowly for 15 minutes, stirring to break up clumps of meat.

Add the garlic, rosemary, bay leaf, and black pepper to the pan. Stir well and cook for 10 minutes over medium heat. Stir in the wine, cover, and cook for an additional 10 minutes. Using the back of a large slotted spoon, mash any chunks in the sauce until fine. Add the canned and fresh tomatoes and the nutmeg. Remove the bay leaf and discard. Add the boiling water and cook, uncovered, for 45 minutes at a simmer. Serve this sauce with a thicker pasta, such as rigatoni or spaghetti, or use it to make lasagna.

Note: This recipe can easily be doubled.

Makes about 4 cups sauce

Venda's Pesto Sauce

2 cups extra-virgin olive oil

2 cups fresh Italian (flat-leaf) parsley

6 cloves garlic

½ cups pine nuts (pignoli)

1 teaspoon freshly ground black pepper

1 teaspoon salt

1 cup freshly grated cheese, Pecorino Romano

½ cup water

2 firmly packed cups fresh basil leaves

Place all the ingredients, except the basil, in a blender or food processor. Puree until smooth. Add the basil in batches and puree until it becomes a creamy pesto sauce. Additional salt and pepper may be added to suit your taste. This amount of sauce is enough for 1 pound of dried pasta.

Makes 2 pints

Venda's Cosimo's Famous Pizza

4 pounds pizza dough (available at any supermarket)

1 tablespoon Crisco

1 (32-ounce) can whole, peeled Italian tomatoes, preferably San Marzano

1 teaspoon salt

Pinch of freshly ground black pepper

1 teaspoon dried oregano

1 teaspoon finely chopped garlic

½ cup extra-virgin olive oil

2 pounds shredded mozzarella cheese

To prepare the dough: Coat a large sheet pan (approximately 18 x 24 inches in size) or two quarter-sheet pans (approximately 12 x 9 inches in size) with Crisco. Place the dough in the center of the pan. (If using two smaller pans, divide the dough in two and then place in the center of each pan.) Work the dough out to the outside edges of the pan(s). The dough should be about ½-inch thick, except for the border which should be about 1-inch thick. Place the sheet pan(s) in the refrigerator for 30 minutes.

Preheat the oven to 400°F.

To prepare the sauce: Place the tomatoes in a large bowl. With your hands, break up the tomatoes to a pulp. Add the salt, pepper, oregano, garlic, and olive oil. Using a spoon, blend until all the ingredients are well mixed.

To assemble the pizza: Remove the sheet pan(s) from refrigerator. Pour the sauce in center of dough and spread out covering the pizza but leaving a half-inch border. Sprinkle the mozzarella cheese generously over the entire pizza.

Place sheet pan(s) in the oven and bake for 45 to 60 minutes, depending on your oven. Check after 45 minutes. The pizza is done when the cheese is bubbly and the crust around the edges is golden brown.

Venda's Lobster and Asparagus Agnolotti

1 pound fresh or frozen lobster and asparagus agnolotti (see note)

Sauce

2 tablespoons extra-virgin olive oil

1 garlic clove, minced

½ teaspoon red pepper flakes

8 littleneck clams, preferably Rhode Island, well rinsed

6 large shrimp, peeled, preferably with heads still attached

½ cup white wine

1 small ripe plum (Roma) tomato, diced

1 tablespoon chopped fresh Italian (flat-leaf) parsley

In a pot of boiling salted water, cook the agnolotti according to directions on the package.

In a large sauté pan, heat the olive oil over medium-high heat. Add the garlic and sauté until golden — be careful not to burn it. Add the red pepper flakes, clams, and shrimp. (The shrimp cook quickly, so watch carefully.) Once the clams have opened and the shrimp have turned pink in color, add the white wine and diced tomatoes and cook over medium heat. Once the wine has evaporated, add the chopped parsley. Drain the agnolotti and place on a serving dish. Pour the sauce over the agnolotti and serve.

Note: Agnolotti is a type of stuffed pasta, similar in size to ravioli and tortellini. It is available fresh or frozen at Italian markets.

Note: This dish can easily be doubled to serve 4 people.

Serves 2

"You often find that the best soup is cooked in a small pot."
Italian proverb

Philadelphia, Pennsylvania's 9th Street Italian Market

The city of Philadelphia was founded by William Penn in 1682. Originally inhabited by the Lenape Indians, Philadelphia, the "City of Brotherly Love," was a place where people could live without fear of religious persecution, and, as a result, Quakers, Mennonites, and others came to the city for refuge. As Philadelphia grew into a major political and economic center — by 1800 it was the largest city in the United States — people of many religions and ethnicities flocked to the city. During the nineteenth and twentieth centuries, immigration and migration led to large concentrations of Germans, Italians, Irish, Asians, Puerto Ricans, and African Americans. Even today, Philadelphia is still a major center for immigration.

The Italian immigrants — tradesmen, scholars, entrepreneurs, and artists — began to arrive in the mid-1800s. They settled in South Philadelphia and established the new community known as "Little Italy." In 1852, the community organized the first Italian national parish in the United States, St. Mary Magdalene de Pazzi Church, which still stands at 8th and Montrose Streets. Though there were Italians living in Philadelphia before the Revolutionary War, it wasn't until the 1850s that the community created a sense of belonging for the larger wave of immigrants. By 1900, Italians were the largest

Vintage map of Philadelphia, Pennsylvania circa 1875 (courtesy of Library of Congress)

immigrant group in Philadelphia and Little Italy in South Philadelphia was the second largest Italian American community in the United States — second only to New York City's Little Italy.

There is not just one neighborhood in Philadelphia's Little Italy, but twelve, and each one has a uniqueness all its own. Some of the neighborhoods, such as Belle Vista, Capitolo, Columbus Square, and Tolentine, are tourist-friendly and offer shopping and dining. Some of the best Italian restaurants lie in the neighborhoods of Epiphany, East Oregon, and Santa Monica. The strictly residential Italian neighborhoods include Stella Maris, Girard Estates, Moyamensing, Packer Park, and South Brook Park. But all of these neighborhoods are still bound by the Italian culture that influences every aspect of their lives — through food, music, and family.

As with all Italian American communities, the residents of Philadelphia's Little Italy made great contributions to the culture of the city. Most landmarks were built, tiled, bricked, or painted by the newly arrived immigrants. One of the most enduring and celebrated contributions to Philadelphia is the 9th Street Italian Market. The area took off as an Italian hub in the mid-to-late 1880s when Antonio Palumbo began housing hundreds of Italian immigrants in his boardinghouse. He made it possible for the immigrants to begin a new life in Philadelphia by encouraging them to become merchants, selling meats, produce, fruits, and other items along 9th Street, between Catherine and Wharton Streets. The Italian Market was born!

Today, the heart of South Philadelphia is the over 100-year-old Italian Market, which bills itself as the oldest and largest working outdoor market in the United States. It

consists of ten blocks (along 9th Street and the surrounding neighborhood) of Italian eateries, and some of the best quality bakeries, butcher shops, and fruit stands in the city. Strolling beneath the bright metal awnings of third- and fourth-generation family-owned shops, you are taken back to a simpler but more gregarious time when families shopped for meats and poultry at the now 100-year-old Esposito's, meticulously selected their fruits and vegetables from Giordano's, which has been there since 1900, all the while visiting with old friends. Though much different in flavor from the other communities, it was and still is a place of raucous fun, with merchants singing, yelling, and sometimes insulting the customers to force them to either buy something or just go away. The market's rich history, coupled with its carnival atmosphere and the well-priced goods, are what keep the locals — and tourists from around the world — coming back.

The Victor Café

1303 Dickinson Street, Philadelphia

(courtesy of The Victor Café)

Classical music and more importantly, Grand Opera (a genre of nineteenth-century opera) was the great love of John DiStefano when he immigrated to the United States from a village near Naples in 1908. Settling in Philadelphia he opened a gramophone store in 1918 where his friends and family, and anyone interested in music, would come to spend time and listen to newly recorded operas, symphonies, and popular music. John became an advisor and confidant for musicians and singers anxious to break into the music business. John would often take the South Street Ferry to the RCA Victor recording studio located across the river in Camden, New Jersey where he would meet with directors, arrange auditions, and make suggestions for future recordings. His expertise in vocal repertoire and voice was highly valued and therefore when Mr. DiStefano would make a suggestion, it was taken.

One of his most prized discoveries was, Alfred Arnold Cocozza, a local patron who would come into the gramophone shop. One day, John took him across the Delaware River. A recording contract was signed and that artist became known as Mario Lanza, a popular American tenor and movie star. With the repeal of Prohibition in 1933, John was able to purchase a liquor license, transforming DiStefano's Gramophone Shop into The Victor Café — the "music lover's rendezvous."

His effort to bring together artists and musicians was already legend; now, with the café, he would be able to combine his two loves — food and music — and become known for his prowess as a café owner as well. Not only would the opera be wonderful, but the food would be mouthwatering too.

Over time, Armand and Henry, John's two sons, took over the operation of the café. John died in 1954 and eventually Henry took over full responsibility of the café. After his death in 1986, his wife and children kept The Victor Café running.

Today, the family continues to share with their customers the feeling of living a part of history and customers enjoy hearing memories of the four generations of family members still involved in the café. Their food is as good as it gets.

Over the years, John's family collected hundreds of photographs of famous and not-so-famous artists as well as a collection of thousands of 78 rpm recordings, many of them rare or out of print and some never even published.

As a tribute to the famous RCA Victor recording company, Nipper (the well-known mascot of "His Master's Voice" fame) is prominent at the front door, offering diners a preview of what awaits them. In years past, live performances of instrumental solos, arias, poetry readings, or soliloquies would be performed by the patrons. In 1979, amateur opera singers were hired as wait staff and a new tradition was established. On a shelf between the two rooms of the café sits a bell that is rung every twenty minutes, signaling a performance to be enjoyed by eager diners. Close your eyes, and you just might be listening to a future Enrico Caruso, Mario Lanza, or Luciano Pavarotti.

The Victor Café Veal, Chicken or Turkey Marsala

8 (4-ounce) veal, chicken or turkey cutlets,
   pounded to ⅛-inch thick

All-purpose flour, for dredging

2 tablespoons extra-virgin olive oil

1 tablespoon butter (optional)

5 chopped cloves garlic

1 cup Marsala wine, plus 2 tablespoons to deglaze pan

1 cup sliced mushrooms

Salt and pepper, to taste

Chopped fresh Italian (flat-leaf) parsley, for garnish (optional)

Lightly dredge the meat cutlets in flour and shake off excess flour. In 10-inch skillet, heat the olive oil and butter, if using, over medium-high heat. Add the garlic and sauté until lightly browned. Sauté the meat, a few pieces at a time, until lightly browned on both sides. Add the Marsala wine and mushrooms, reduce the heat to medium, and cook 2 to 3 minutes, or until mushrooms are softened. Remove the meat and mushrooms to platter and sprinkle on salt and pepper. Keep warm in a very low oven.

To the skillet, add the remaining 2 tablespoons of Marsala and simmer over medium heat, while stirring to loosen the pan drippings, until the alcohol cooks off, about 3 minutes. Pour over the meat and sprinkle with the chopped parsley. If the sauce has become too thick, add some chicken broth or stock to thin it. Serve with a medley of sautéed carrots, zucchini, and tomatoes.

Serves 4

Exterior of the Victor Record Shop and Café. From left to right: Dominick DiStefano, Henry DiStefano, John DiStefano and Gina Valente, circa 1930s (courtesy of Pat DiStefano)

Dante & Luigi's

762 South Tenth Street, Philadelphia

Dante & Luigi's is one of the oldest existing Italian restaurants in the U.S. Established in 1899, it is still located in its original spot — two adjoining, 153-year-old, converted townhouses in the Bella Vista neighborhood of Philadelphia.

Five generations of the DiRocco family operated the restaurant, which also once had a second-story rooming house for incoming immigrants. The immigrants would arrive, unable to speak English, with just a note pinned to their lapels sending them to Dante & Luigi's, where they were given lodging and a job in the restaurant or in the newly established Italian market section of Philadelphia.

The restaurant is a staple of Old World charm and ambience. The list of celebrities who have dined here is long and includes the likes of Vice

President Joe Biden, Vic Damone, Al Martino, Peter Coyote, Melissa Manchester as well as the cast of *The Sopranos*. The new owners, Connie and Michael LaRussa, purchased the restaurant fifteen years ago and although it's not a rooming house any longer, it is situated in what has become an integral part of the now upscale urban area known as Center City Philadelphia.

(courtesy of Dante & Luigi's)

(courtesy of Dante & Luigi's)

Dante & Luigi's Clams & Spaghetti Marinara

3 tablespoons extra-virgin olive oil

1½ tablespoons sliced garlic

1½ tablespoons minced onion

Pinch of red pepper flakes, or to taste

48 littleneck clams, well-rinsed

1 cup white wine

1 cup fish stock

20 leaves of fresh basil

Pinch of salt and black pepper, or to taste

¾ cup marinara sauce

1 pound dried spaghetti or linguini

Bring a large pot of salted water to a boil.

In a 10 to 12-inch sauté pan, heat the oil over medium heat. Add the garlic and onion and sauté for 2 minutes, until browned. Add the red pepper flakes and the clams and sauté for another 3 minutes.

Deglaze the pan with the white wine and cook over medium heat until the liquid is reduced by half. Add the fish stock and cook for 3 minutes more. Add the basil, salt, pepper, and marinara sauce and cook for 3 to 6 minutes, or until all of the clams have opened. (Discard any clams that did not open.)

While the clams are cooking, add the pasta to the boiling, salted water and cook until al dente. Drain well.

Pour the clam sauce over the pasta and mangia!

Serves 4

(courtesy of Dante & Luigi's)

Philadelphia, Pennsylvania's Italian Market | **149**

Di Bruno Bros.

930 S. 9th Street, Philadelphia

Di Bruno Bros. is part of the fabric of Philadelphia and the fabric of Philadelphia is part of Di Bruno Bros. When you step into this venerable Italian gourmet food shop, you can sense the loyalty between proprietor and customer. Di Bruno Bros. opened its doors in 1939 on 9th Street in the Italian Market in Philadelphia, and respect for the customer was and still is paramount for the owners. Always well-dressed and wearing a tie, Danny, one of the founding brothers, expected professionalism from all his employees, including family members.

In 1935, Danny and Joe Di Bruno emigrated from Abruzzi to the United States when they were just fifteen and sixteen years old. With only a third-grade education, they forged a life in the Italian Market, living in a boarding house, working for street vendors, and then in a butcher shop. When Joe was abruptly fired from his job at one of the major retailers in the Italian Market, his brother Danny also walked out. They went directly across the street and established Di Bruno Bros. Unfortunately, their former employer tried to make it difficult for the Di Brunos to do business, so, in typical entrepreneurial fashion, Danny, armed with a gun, visited the former employer and accused him of taking food from his family's table. With that problem resolved, the Di Brunos, in an effort to respect other grocers, did their best to vary their product line with more diverse gourmet products.

In the mid1960s, they stopped carrying general grocery store items to become the first market to bring specialty products to the Italian Market and renamed the store, Di Bruno Bros. — The House of Cheese. Today the Di Bruno Bros. carries only the highest-quality products, including one of the best prosciuttos in the world — the prosciutto di Parma produced by the artisans at Greci & Folzani in Parma, Italy.

The brothers are proud of their name and over the years have never compromised it by growing the business too large. During downturns in the

Danny Di Bruno (courtesy of Di Bruno Bros.)

economy, they grew deeper rather than wider by working harder and taking less. When Jimmy Buffet, Jack Nicholson, or even President Obama shop here for gourmet cheeses, meats, and pastas, they are now greeted by third-generation Bill Mignucci Jr. and his cousin, Emilio Mignucci, along with countless nephews who took the helm in the 1990s.

Philadelphia is a neighborhood city and great food, along with great sports and great history, are integral parts of the life there. The Di Brunos feel a keen responsibility to their community. In keeping with the traditions of the past, the façade of the market has remained unchanged and the service is still stellar. Philadelphians, the Di Brunos observe, are not the type to look for the latest trends.

The store's Italian Market location (courtesy of Di Bruno Bros.)

Danny (left) and Joe Di Bruno (right) (courtesy of Di Bruno Bros.)

Di Bruno Bros. Prosciutto di Parma

Pig. Salt. Air. Time.

Official Italian law mandates that these are the only ingredients that can be used in the production of prosciutto di Parma. These laws, while seemingly restrictive, enable a broad range of quality which varies from producer to producer.

The Pig

There is no restriction regarding where the pigs are raised— they may come from an Italian province, from the Piedmont to the Veneto and as far south as Tuscany and Emila Romagna. Naturally, the diet of a pig, and even the air it breathes, will vary from region to region, and this difference is imparted in prosciutto di Parma. The dry curing stage amplifies the flavor of each pig — it does not initiate it.

And while the guidelines of the law dictate that the weight of the leg must be a minimum of ten kilograms at harvest, some producers allow the pig to grow larger, which also creates difference in quality. Larger-size legs allow the meat to remain moist, delicate, and sweet during the long curing process.

The Salt

Italian law has no stipulations as to type or amount of salt used in Prosciutto and that allows a producer the ability to use any amount available. When high-quality sea salt is used, Sicilian sea salt being one of the most renowned, the result is prosciutto with amplified flavor and lower salt content — often a third lower. Sea salt, with its extra "salty" flavor, is more efficient at seasoning foods than other types of salt and, therefore, less is needed, which allows the flavor of the food to shine through.

The Air and Time

The air. While prosciutto can be produced anywhere in Italy, the climate of certain areas have long been recognized to produce the best prosciutto. Parma is one of those places. Each distinct region has a Protected Designation of Origin (PDO), and the PDO for Parma waxes poetic about that region: "The breeze, which comes in from the Mediterranean on the Versilia coast, gently blows through the olive and pine trees of the Magra Valley. It then becomes drier as it rushes over the Apennine pass. It acquires the heady fragrance of the chestnut trees before it blows among the hams in the Parma valleys."

The time. The law requires a minimum aging period of ten months. However, many producers will age their hams for longer, some up to two years, which creates an unmatched depth and subtly of flavor.

Ralph's Italian Restaurant

760 S. 9th Street, Philadelphia

In 1893, when Francesco and Catherine Dispigno along with their baby son Ralph, immigrated to America from the island of Ischia, off the coast of Naples, and settled in the Italian enclave around 9th Avenue and Catherine Street, the population was bursting with immigrants of all nationalities looking to make America their home. A fisherman by trade in Italy, Francesco opened his first restaurant in 1900 on Montrose Street where he and his family worked long and hard to achieve success. His son, Ralph, for whom the restaurant was named, was needed at the restaurant and so at the age of fifteen he left school to work there full-time, beginning what would be a long-term commitment to the family business.

RALPH'S
Italian Restaurant
"Oldest Family-Owned Restaurant in America"

760 S. 9th Street • Philadelphia, PA 19147
(215) 627-6011 • Fax (215) 627-6527
E-mail: RalphsRest@aol.com
www.ralphsrestaurant.com

(courtesy of Ralph's Italian Restaurant)

A boarding house on 9th Street, built in the 1880s, became available and in 1915 the Dispignos moved the restaurant to that location, which is where it remains to this day. The family converted two floors of the boarding house to dining space and purchased another house next door for their residence. The third floor of the restaurant was used as a boarding house for newly arrived immigrants who Francesco Dispigno sponsored.

Francesco was successful and his son followed in his footsteps becoming a prosperous businessman in his own right, taking charge of the day-to-day operation of the restaurant. However, in the crash of 1929, Ralph lost everything but the business. In order to survive, Ralph and his wife, Mary, were forced to sell spaghetti and meatballs for five cents from the front door. This hard work and dedication was a testament to the Dispigno family's determination.

When Francesco passed away in the early 1930s, Ralph was well-prepared to continue on and the restaurant has continued to be family-owned and operated for over 100 years. As years passed, Ralph's six children all worked in the restaurant business, sacrificing other careers for the sake of the family. Jimmy Rubino, Jr. and Eddie, the great grandsons of Francesco, are now in charge.

Ralph's has been cooking and serving savory veal, chicken, and pasta dishes throughout the terms of nineteen American presidents, including Theodore Roosevelt who was a customer at the turn of the twentieth century. Other celebrities who have dined here included Frank Sinatra, Tony Bennett, James Darren, Frankie Avalon, Lena Horne, Al Martino,

Francesco Dispigno, circa 1894 (courtesy of Ralph's Italian Restaurant)

Sylvester Stallone, and countless sports stars.

Italian restaurants pride themselves on their veal, and in this respect, Ralph's is king. All the recipes have been handed down from the early 1900s, and the Veal Capricciosa is as mouth-watering today as it was when it was first served. Another 100 years wouldn't be a bad idea!

Ralph's Roasted Garlic Soup

22 cloves garlic (from about 3 heads)

½ cup extra-virgin olive oil, plus extra to coat garlic cloves

1 large onion, preferably Spanish, chopped

3 (28-ounce) cans whole, peeled Italian tomatoes, crushed by hand

2 cups heavy cream

12 fresh basil leaves, chopped

Salt and black pepper, to taste

½ cup chopped fresh Italian (flat-leaf) parsley, for garnish

Preheat the oven to 400°F.

Coat 16 of the garlic cloves with olive oil and place on a sheet pan. Roast the garlic for 40 minutes.

While the garlic is roasting, prepare the soup. Using the side of a large knife, crush the remaining 6 cloves of garlic.

In a 4-quart stockpot, heat the ½ cup of olive oil over medium heat. Add the onion and crushed garlic and cook until the onion is transparent and garlic is turning a golden color. Add the crushed tomatoes and bring to a boil. Reduce the heat to low and cook for 40 minutes, stirring frequently. Add the cream, basil, salt, and black pepper, and cook another 15 minutes.

To serve, divide the soup among four large soup bowls. Add 4 roasted garlic cloves and a generous spoonful of chopped parsley to each bowl. Serve with toasted Italian bread.

Serves 4

Ralph's Sicilian Calamari

2 pounds calamari, cleaned

3 cups all-purpose flour

1¼ cups extra-virgin olive oil

3 hot cherry peppers, sliced

2 pimentos, julienned

½ cup black and green pitted olives

¼ cup capers

2 tablespoons butter

½ cup Sauterne wine

Salt and black pepper, to taste

¼ cup fresh chopped Italian (flat-leaf) parsley

Cut the calamari bodies into 1-inch rings, but leave the tentacles whole. Combine the calamari with the flour in a mixing bowl, tossing the calamari until all of it is coated.

In a large nonstick skillet, heat 1 cup of the olive oil over medium-high heat. Add the calamari and fry in batches until golden brown, about 1 minute. (Do not overcrowd the pan.) Remove with a slotted spoon and set aside.

In another nonstick skillet, heat the remaining ¼ cup of olive oil over medium heat. When the oil is hot, add the hot cherry peppers, pimentos, black and green olives, and capers. When ingredients start to simmer, add the butter and the wine. Once the ingredients start simmering again, toss the calamari into pan with salt and pepper. Stir until the calamari is coated with the ingredients. Serve in large bowl and garnish with the chopped parsley.

Serves 4

"The Family, 2000"

(courtesy of Ralph's Italian Restaurant)

"Eating without drinking is like thunder without the rain."

Italian proverb

Chicago, Illinois's Little Italy

In the 1880s, the hub of Chicago's Little Italy was Taylor Street; it was the destination for many of the city's Italian immigrants who arrived during that time. Chicago was rapidly growing, and by 1890, the immigrant population was at more than 40 percent of all residents and a half million more were added by the end of the decade bringing the population to more than one million. Chicago's Little Italy quickly became the second-largest Italian enclave after New York City.

Taylor Street was also the location of the legendary Hull House. Created by friends Jane Addams and Ellen Gates Starr, Hull House provided social and educational opportunities for working class European immigrants. The Italian community was further aided through the efforts of Mother Cabrini, who helped to establish and maintain hospitals and schools for the Italian immigrants not only in Chicago but throughout the United States. Her efforts earned her the title of the Patron Saint of Immigrants.

Although new jobs in manufacturing lured immigrants to the surrounding communities, many remained in the Taylor Street neighborhood. A mile or so south, Oakley and 24th Street became home to the immigrants from Tuscany who worked at the McCormick Reaper plant. In 1880, the famous (or infamous as it was later thought) planned company town established by George Pullman became home to many Italian brick makers. North of the city, the Highwood community, which was developed after the turn of the century, welcomed immigrants from Modena who moved there from the Illinois coal towns. The town of Blue Island at the southwest border of the city was heavily settled by railroad laborers. Chicago Heights, thirty miles south of the Loop, had a population that was 50 percent Italian by 1920 and Melrose Park, to the west, was a place of second settlement, attracting Italians from the inner city to the suburbs.

Melrose Park became known as the quintessential Italian suburb in Chicago. One of the reasons was Our Lady of Mount Carmel church, located In Melrose Park, founded in 1903. The church's annual Feast is a celebration held every July since 1893 and attracts thousands of visitors.

Chicago's Italian community is still haunted by the most famous Italian American criminal, Al Capone. Capone's life illustrated a true love/hate relationship with the citizens of Chicago. He operated a vice, gambling, and illegal liquor empire — managed with the "consent" (gained through bribes to officials) of the city's non-Italian political leadership — while simultaneously fancying himself to be a modern-day Robin Hood as he passed out cash at social functions and established soup kitchens for the poor.

Though the numbers directly involved in syndicate crime were less than 1 percent of the Italian American people, the Capone mob captured the imagination of journalists and moviemakers who have helped to sustain the negative stereotype that continues sixty-three years after Capone's death.

The all too common, sad, and frustrating story of urban renewal schemes in the 1960s, when the city of Chicago took a swath of land from this tightly-knit Italian community to make way for the University of Illinois Medical Center, the Eisenhower Expressway, and for public housing, was a huge blow to this charming neighborhood. And, as with so many original Italian American communities, many of the second, third, and fourth generations have moved to the suburbs, but their familial and emotional ties to the neighborhood remain strong. The attempt and success at rebirth came a few years later with the establishment of The Italian American Boxing Hall of Fame and, a year later in 1978, with the birth of the National Italian American Sports Hall of Fame honoring the likes of Eddie Arcaro, Joe DiMaggio, and Vince Lombardi. The presence of these national treasures, as well as a rebirth of charming restaurants and cafés, assures that the heart of Little Italy in Chicago is as strong as it was a century ago.

The "original" Ferrara Bakery located on Taylor St. in Chicago (courtesy of Nella Davy)

Tony Nitti's Bar-B-Que

3131 W. Armitage Avenue, Chicago

Many immigrant stories begin with a small pushcart evolving into the ownership of a grocery store and then, eventually, a restaurant. But in this case, the story is reversed.

Anthony and Angela Nitti were olive growers in their native Bari, a province in the southern Italian region of Puglia. They prided themselves on growing the largest olives in the region and it is believed that one of the original trees they planted is still producing olives.

When Anthony Nitti put his son on a ship to America, Joe Nitti had no idea that his father sent him to the United States without the knowledge of his mother, Angela. He would never again see his family.

He arrived at the port of Boston Harbor and moved to Chicago to live with relatives. His first love was music, and in particular drums, which he pursued with a passion. Eventually he formed his own band, "Joe Nitti & His Orchestra."

Joe married and had four children and happily his son, Tony, showed an entrepreneurial interest

Tony Nitti (courtesy of Tony Nitti)

in business. As a young boy, Tony was already operating a pushcart selling bananas on the streets of Chicago. But it was in 1948, at age nineteen, that Tony, along with his father, Joe, opened Nitti's Bar-B-Que in the Grand and Ogden district of Chicago — one of the smaller Barese Italian-American communities in Illinois. It is no secret that Chicago supplies some of the best meat throughout the United States and Tony's brother, Leroy, known as the best meat man in Chicago, was there to supply the meat.

The Bar-B-Que restaurant lasted only two years

Tony Nitti (courtesy of Tony Nitti)

because the restaurant across the street gave them an offer that they couldn't refuse. They sold Nitti's Bar-B-Que and soon after started a small chain of markets called Nitti's Certified Super-Mart, delivering groceries and such in 1952. Nitti's is a thing of the past with the building demolished and the neighborhood is devoid of aromatic basil and tomatoes as a new and hopeful immigrant culture has moved in. No longer will one see the delivery trucks around the neighborhood, but with the older residents, the memories still linger.

Tony Nitti's Chicago Wedding Soup with Tiny Meatballs

Meatballs

½ pound ground beef

2 tablespoons grated Romano cheese

2 egg yolks

Scant ¼ teaspoon salt

1 slice bread, soaked in water and squeezed dry

2 teaspoons fresh chopped parsley

4 cups beef broth (recipe follows)

½ cup acini di pepe (fine soup pasta)

2 tablespoons grated Romano cheese, for serving

To make the meatballs: Thoroughly mix together by hand the ingredients for the meatballs in a bowl. Shape the mixture into small meatballs, about the size of marbles.

To make the soup: Bring the broth to boil, add the soup pasta and little meatballs and cook gently about 7 minutes, or until pasta is cooked to your liking. Divide among four soup bowls and serve with grated Romano cheese.

Serves 4

Beef Broth

1 pound beef chuck

1 good marrow bone

3 quarts cold water

3 stalks celery

1 small onion

2 carrots

3 fresh tomatoes, cut into pieces, or one-half 14.5-ounce can whole, peeled tomatoes, drained and cut or broken into pieces

1 teaspoon salt

½ teaspoon black pepper

Place the meat, bone, and cold water in a large stock pot and bring to a boil. Remove any residue that forms on top of the water. Add the celery, onion, carrots, and tomatoes. Cover the pot and cook over medium heat for about 1¼ hours, or until the meat is tender. Remove the meat and use as desired. Strain the broth. A little water may be added if the broth seems too condensed.

(Makes 2 quarts)

Italian Beef

1 (3 to 4-pound) boneless rump or round roast

6 cloves garlic, cut into slivers

1 cup water

1 tablespoon salt

1 tablespoon coarsely ground black pepper

1 tablespoon crushed red pepper flakes

1 tablespoon dried oregano

6 to 8 long Italian rolls (or "hoagie," "sub," or "grinder" rolls) or other rolls of your choice, for serving

Preheat the oven to 250°F.

Make slits all over the roast with the tip of a knife and insert the garlic slivers. Place the roast and water in a Dutch oven or other deep-sided pan not much larger than the roast. Pour in the water and sprinkle the seasonings over top. Cover tightly and bake 2 hours, basting occasionally. Remove from the pan and let rest until cool enough to handle. Slice very thinly. Add a little water to the pan and stir until the cooked juices and seasonings are well mixed. Put the sliced beef back into the pan and reheat.

To serve, slice the roll of your choice lengthwise and place meat on top, spooning more of the juice on top. The meat may be topped with hot or sweet Gardinara, a spicy blend of pickled hot peppers, celery, carrots, cauliflower, assorted spices in vinaigrette It's a Chicago thing! (**Note:** Gardinara can be purchased in 16-, 18- or 32-ounce jars.)

Serves 6 to 8

Chicago-Style Sausage & Pepper Sandwiches

2 to 2½ pounds hot or sweet Italian sausage

¼ cup water

2 green bell peppers, cut into 2-inch-long strips

1 (14.5-ounce) can whole, peeled Italian tomatoes, drained and chopped

1 teaspoon garlic salt

¼ teaspoon black pepper

6 long Italian rolls (or "hoagie," "sub," or "grinder" rolls)

Place the sausages and the water in a large, skillet or brasier pan and cook, covered, over medium heat for 10 minutes. When the water has cooked off, the sausages will begin to brown. Turn the sausage occasionally to brown them evenly. Make sure the sausages are thoroughly cooked through.

Remove the sausage from the pan and drain off excess grease. Return the sausage to the pan and add the green peppers, tomatoes, garlic salt, and pepper. Bring to a boil. Reduce the heat to low and cook for 15 to 20 minutes. Place the sausages in 6 split Italian rolls and spoon the peppers and sauce over top.

Serves 6

Chicago-Style Pizza

1 recipe Chicago-Style Pizza Dough (recipe follows)
   or 1 pound store-bought pizza dough

All-purpose flour, for dusting work surface

2 tablespoons cornmeal

Extra-virgin olive oil

1 (8-ounce) can tomato sauce

1 tablespoon dried basil

1 tablespoon dried oregano

½ teaspoon garlic salt

½ teaspoon black pepper

1 pound mozzarella, shredded

2 ounces Romano cheese, grated (½ cup)

Optional Toppings

1 pound hot or sweet Italian sausage

Mushrooms, sliced

Green bell pepper, sliced

If using sausage as a topping, remove the sausage from its casing and break it into small pieces. In a large skillet over medium heat, fry the sausage until well cooked. Remove from the pan and drain on paper towels. Break into very small pieces or grind.

Preheat the oven to 450°F.

To shape the pizza dough, divide the dough in half. Working on a floured surface, roll the dough halves into two 12-inch circles, if using a pizza stone, or into two oblong shapes, about 10 x 14 inches each, if using a large cookie sheet. Sprinkle the pizza stone or baking sheet with 1 tablespoon of the cornmeal. Place the prepared pizza dough on the cornmeal and brush the top very lightly with olive oil.

In a small bowl, combine the tomato sauce, basil, oregano, garlic salt, and pepper. Evenly spread half of the sauce over the pizza dough. Top with half of the cheeses and add any additional toppings of your choice. Drizzle some olive oil on the top. Bake until the crust is brown around the edges and the cheese is bubbly, about 20 to 25 minutes minutes. Repeat with the remaining pizza dough, sauce, cheese and toppings, if using.

Makes two 12-inch pizzas

Chicago-Style Pizza Dough
(Tony Nitti's BBQ)

1 cup warm water, about 100°F

¼ teaspoon sugar

¼ ounce (1 envelope) active dry yeast

3 cups unbleached, all-purpose flour

1 teaspoon salt

1 tablespoon extra-virgin olive oil

In a small bowl, combine ¼ cup of the warm water with the sugar and yeast. Let stand in warm place for 10 minutes. The yeast will begin to form bubbles.

In a large bowl, combine the flour and salt. Make a well in the flour and add the proofed yeast mixture and remaining ¾ cup of warm water and the olive oil. Mix the dry and liquid ingredients together with your hands, and then turn the mixture out onto a lightly floured work surface. Knead the mixture, turning and folding, for 5 to 8 minutes or until dough becomes smooth and elastic. Put the dough into a clean bowl, cover with a cloth and let rise in a warm place (about 75 to 80°F) for 1 to 2 hours, until doubled in size.

Punch the dough down with your fist and knead 1 minute. The dough is now ready to be shaped, following the instructions in the recipe for Chicago-Style Pizza.

Makes two 12-inch pizzas

GUARINO'S
RESTAURANT
LIQUORS

BENVENUTO

LA PICCOLA ITALIA

CHOCOLATES

MAYFIELD
SMOKE SHOP

GARDEN
OPEN

"Eat with gusto but drink in moderation."
Italian proverb

Cleveland, Ohio's Murray Hill

Like many Italian communities in America, the one in Cleveland, Ohio has evolved over the years. In its early days in the 1890s, it was a cohesive and somewhat insular enclave, centered around what was then known as "Big Italy" in the Haymarket section, the center of the city's produce markets. As the neighborhood deteriorated, the Italian residents moved to better housing in the Murray Hill section of Cleveland, which became known as Little Italy. This neighborhood was made up of marble workers, monument carvers, landscapers, sewer workers, and bridge, railway and streetcar builders, and it proved to be the most enduring of Cleveland's six Italian communities. Some of these other communities were populated by Neapolitan immigrants, who were skilled artisans specializing in embroidery, lacework, and tailoring, and worked in the city's thriving garment business.

One of the local celebrities who put Cleveland's Little Italy on the map was Hector Boiardi. In 1924, he opened his restaurant, Il Giardino d'Italia, where his spaghetti sauce was so popular that he began selling it in milk bottles. Demand soared and Boiardi built a factory in 1928 to produce an inexpensive, pre-packaged line of meals that could be made at home — and that's how Chef Boyardee products were introduced to the world. Chef Hector's image still adorns the cans of this famous brand.

Opposite page: Guarino's store front (courtesy of Guarino's)

Eventually, the disparate Italian communities would all fold into Murray Hill, bringing with them a strong sense of national identity. In keeping with their devoted connection to their roots, they brought with them the values and dialects from their villages in Italy. Our Lady of the Most Holy Rosary Catholic Church, built in 1892, and the Alta House, a community organization founded in 1895 by John D. Rockefeller, are what hold this community together to this day. Murray Hill's Little Italy is a bustling neighborhood today, and restaurants and galleries can be found all along Mayfield Road — its main artery — and their annual festival, the Feast of the Assumption, draws residents from all over Cleveland, proving that this Little Italy is still alive and vital.

Bread baker, circa 1920 (courtesy of DiCamillo Baking Co.)

Guarino's

12309 Mayfield Road, Cleveland

The history Guarino's Restaurant in the Little Italy section of Cleveland would not be complete without the story of the enormous flowering trumpet vine that still grows in the back garden of the restaurant — it is the stuff of legend.

In 1918, Vincenzo (Jimmy) Guarino and his brother emigrated from Sicily to Cleveland, Ohio, where they worked paving the streets and carving monument stones. Within a short time, Jimmy bought a building that had previously been a bar. Behind the bar grew magnificent trumpet and grape vines, which had been brought to America in 1898 from Sicily. Before long, Jimmy was harvesting the grapes and making wine. These vines, which would be important in the lives of many people, covered the entire back portion of his yard as well as a shared yard with their neighbors, the Lomparos.

During this time, young Mary Lomparo was mourning the death of her father and her mother was preparing to deliver another child. Her father had not yet been buried and his glass-top coffin was still available for viewing at Lake View, the cemetery just up the road. Mary worried that if

(courtesy of Guarino's)

she didn't take her new sibling to view the coffin (a superstitious practice in Italian culture that promised a good life), that things would not be good for the family. She struggled with the decision, but in the end she decided not to bring the baby to the viewing. Mary's decision proved to be the right one as her life turned out to be a happy one. She went on to marry her next door neighbor, Jimmy, in April of 1918 and she worked with him in the bar and soon-to-be restaurant.

Mary knew there was potential in the place, but she grew frustrated as she watched patrons go into the bar, shoot pool, drink wine, and end up being a neighborhood nuisance. Mary was not without ambitions of her own and she had an idea to use

(courtesy of Guarino's)

the bounty from her garden to make dishes for Guarino's Liquor and Restaurant. The transformation began as she prepared Sunday dinners for patrons; eventually, the place became so popular that the "bar" became a full-service restaurant.

Mary and Jimmy had three children and one of them, Sam, was childhood friends with a young girl named Nancy Phillips. The friends grew up, married other people, and moved on with their lives but they never lost touch. During the 1980s, when Sam became very ill, he turned to his best friend, Nancy for her help. They never married, but the friendship endured and was rewarding for both of them. Nancy cared for Sam in his remaining years, and he, likewise, provided for her with a portion of his beloved restaurant. Nancy Phillips now owns the restaurant outright and it is her children and grandchildren who lovingly operate Guarino's to this day. On Christmas and Thanksgiving, Nancy personally cooks and feeds the homeless at the restaurant. The wine is no longer made at Guarino's, but the vines are still there and they serve as a reminder of the history and longevity of the restaurant in this tight-knit community and the strength and love that comes from an abiding friendship.

Guarino's Meatballs

Meatballs

3 eggs

1½ tablespoons salt

¼ teaspoon pepper

1½ teaspoons ground sage

½ teaspoon Accent® (msg) (optional)

¼ cup minced onion

1¼ cups breadcrumbs

3½ pounds ground beef

1½ pounds ground pork

Gravy

3 cups water

2 tablespoons all-purpose flour

1½ tablespoons Kitchen Bouquet Browning & Seasoning Sauce®

Preheat the oven to 450°F.

To make the meatballs: Beat the eggs slightly in a large bowl. Add all of the dry seasonings, onion, and breadcrumbs. Stir to combine and let stand until the breadcrumbs soften. Add the ground beef and pork and mix thoroughly by hand.

Using a medium-sized ice cream scoop, form the mixture into balls and place them in a roasting pan. Brown the meatballs in the oven, shaking the pan to turn the meatballs. When the meatballs are browned, remove them from the oven and transfer them to a 9 x 12 lasagna dish. Reduce the oven temperature to 350°F.

To make the gravy: Place the roasting pan used to brown the meatballs on the stovetop over low heat. Sprinkle the flour over the pan drippings while whisking and let cook for 4 to 5 minutes while whisking. Add the water in a slow steady stream, continuously whisking. Bring the liquid to a simmer over medium-high heat, while whisking. Reduce the heat to low and let simmer, whisking frequently, until the sauce is smooth and thick. Stir in the Kitchen Bouquet. Pour over the meat balls, cover, and return to the oven. Bake for 1 hour. These meatballs can be served as a side dish or accompanied with a side of spaghetti.

Makes about 16 large meatballs

Bird's eyeview of Cleveland, Ohio (courtesy of Library of Congress)

Maria's "300"

300 ALBEMARLE STREET
BALTIMORE MD.

"Buy good quality and sell at the market price. "
Italian proverb

Baltimore, Maryland's Little Italy

In the working-class port city of Baltimore, Maryland, where all ethnic groups live and work side by side, the Italians flourished despite some difficult times. Baltimore's Little Italy is a tenacious community, and one of the most populated Little Italys in America. By the turn of the nineteenth century, it was a thriving Italian neighborhood teeming with row houses, Italian restaurants, cafés, and bakeries. The community was located close to the Inner Harbor area and Fells Point where the Italian immigrants who were skilled in fishing and shipbuilding found work. The neighborhood was close-knit and people in the neighborhood took pride in their streets, homes, businesses, and churches. However, the introduction of immigration quotas in 1921 and 1924 slowed Italian immigration measurably. Disaster hit in February, 1904 as the great Baltimore Fire threatened the city. Residents of Little Italy, fearing the fire would come close to their homes, went to the harbor with a statue of St. Anthony, the patron saint of "lost things," and prayed the fire would not cross Jones Falls and endanger their community. Thankfully, the winds died down, the fires subsided, and the Little Italy community was spared. Since that time, the festival of St. Anthony has been held every June to commemorate and honor those who suffered in that tragic, but ultimately, miraculous event.

Opposite page: Menu cover, circa 1960 (courtesy of Maria's 300)

By the end of WWII, the demand for dock and shipyard workers — who were the economic backbone of the community — came to a halt. Machines could easily do the work of dozens of men and by the 1950s the shipping industry abandoned the city. In 1959, more troubles ensued as the area became surrounded by public-housing developments, which often brought drugs and crime. The residents, however, refused to surrender their neighborhood. They were determined to stave off the downturn by supporting their local businesses. Looking to their faith and their family to meet the challenge head on, they stayed strong and survived.

The late 1960s was a period of rebirth for Baltimore and the waterfront in particular. But before long, the next decade brought another menace: a planned freeway project, presented in the guise of "urban renewal," threatened to cut through the middle of Little Italy. Thankfully, due to the intervention of Senator Barbara Mikulski, who was devoted to Baltimore's Little Italy, the plans were scrapped and the neighborhood was once again, secure.

Today, this gentrified neighborhood continues to be host to several restaurants, cafés, and markets. During the warm months of summer, bocce ball is played, festivals are celebrated, and residents and visitors enjoy some of the best food available as they attend Cinema Alfresco, an open-air film event. Italian culture is alive and kicking in Baltimore.

Sabatino's Restaurant

901 Fawn Street, Baltimore

The friendship of two Italian immigrants produced a family legacy of three generations that continues to this day. In 1923, Joseph Canzani emigrated from Palermo, Italy, to the Italian section in Baltimore, Maryland, and worked in nearly all aspects of the food business. For 32 years, he worked as a fruit vendor, a chef, and a grocer. Then, in 1955, luck smiled upon him. In that year, Joseph teamed up with his wealthy friend, Sabatino ("Sabby") Luperini, and together the two men opened Sabatino's, a small 50-seat restaurant in the same location where it stands today. When Sabby retired eleven years later, he left the restaurant to Joe and his family. Over the years, they have enlarged and expanded it to accommodate 450 persons.

Legend has it that some judges from Baltimore who came to Sabatino's for lunch would joke that one of the restaurant's popular salads should have a unique name to reflect the sometimes "under the table" activities taking place there. Hence, the salad of iceberg lettuce, tossed with shrimp, salami, provolone, and their famous cheesy house dressing became known as the "Bookmaker Salad."

Front entrance to Sabatinos, 2005 (courtesy of Sabatino's Restaurant)

Veal Francese a la Sabatino

2 eggs

Pinch of fresh chopped Italian (flat-leaf) parsley

Pinch of salt

Pinch of black pepper

½ cup half-and-half

1½ cups Italian breadcrumbs

1¼ pounds veal scallopine

3 tablespoons butter

4 tablespoons extra-virgin olive oil

2 tablespoons all-purpose flour

¾ cup dry sherry

Juice of ¼ lemon

¾ cup chicken broth

4 slices lemon, for garnish

In a mixing bowl, whisk the eggs until smooth. Add the eggs, parsley, salt, pepper and half-and-half and whisk until smooth. Place the bread crumbs in a separate bowl. Pound each slice of veal between layers of waxed paper until very thin. Dip the veal in the egg batter and then coat both sides with the bread crumbs, shaking off loose breading.

In a heavy skillet, heat the butter and oil over medium-high heat. When hot, add the veal and fry until golden brown, about 2 to 3 minutes per side. Remove veal and set aside on warm platter. Add the flour to pan and stir until brown over medium heat. Stir in the sherry, lemon juice, and chicken broth. Let simmer for 3 minutes. Pour the sauce over the fried veal and garnish with lemon slices.

Serves 4

"Better an egg today than the chicken tomorrow."
Italian proverb

St. Louis's The Hill

La Montagna, or "The Hill,"as it has became known, was as vibrant a neighborhood as any other community of Italian immigrants. Located close to the highest point in St. Louis, and surrounded by clay mines, railroad tracks, factories, and the River Des Peres, The Hill remained remote from the rest of the city, which only solidified the community's strong ethnicity.

It was the pre-Civil War discovery of clay deposits that would eventually bring the Italians to St. Louis. Most were peasants — the *contadini* — from the Lombardy region of Northern Italy. The *contadini* found it difficult to find work in Lombardy, and so when the Big Muddy Coal and Iron Company from Illinois came to Italy to recruit workers, many left in hopes of finding work, but with the belief that it would be temporary. Many soon became disenchanted with the grueling work and eventually made their way from Illinois to Missouri to work in the clay fields, where a major employer of immigrant labor was the Evans and Howard Firebrick Company.

By the end of the nineteenth century, there were more than a dozen tile and brick factories that had grown up along the banks of the River Des Peres, making St. Louis the largest brick manufacturing center in the United States in the early 1900s. The clay products and bricks produced in St. Louis were used to build New York City's Chrysler

Opposite page: Saint Louis, circa 1896 (courtesy of Library of Congress)

Building and Chicago's Navy Pier. Germans, the Irish, and African Americans initially provided the major source of labor for the mines and factories in St. Louis, but, by the time the National Origins Act of 1924 shut the door on immigration from southeastern Europe, the Italian immigrant population had grown and outnumbered the other groups.

The initial Italian immigrant population, arriving at the beginning of the 1880s, was predominately male. The men lived in the Fairmont section of St. Louis in boarding houses within walking distance to the clay fields. Living frugally and earning only meager incomes, they eventually brought their families to the United States. Their hardscrabble, mining camp existence was eventually transformed as the population grew and turned this into a flourishing Italian immigrant neighborhood.

The pattern of group settlement that fueled the influx of Italians from Lombardy, and particularly a tiny village called Cuggiono, was known as the "Great Chain Migration." Letters and return visits by "americani" forged "endless chains," link by link, between Europe and America. This "chain" quickly populated The Hill in St. Louis. The initial hopes of the "birds of passage," those immigrants who expected to return to their homeland after making a living, were often forgotten, as most were content with their new lives in America.

The Lombardi immigrants, who came to the United States between 1880 and 1924, did not, as is often depicted, have a depressing and lonely migration experience. Rather, the cushioned, communal environment of The Hill was the result of extremely strong familial and paesani connections. The immigrants were not uprooted, but transplanted. After 1900, however, Southern Italian immigrants populated The Hill in equal numbers.

180 | America's Little Italys

(courtesy of Rigazzi's)

The Louisiana Purchase Exposition at the 1904 World's Fair in St. Louis was a great achievement for Italians, not only those who lived on The Hill, but for all those who lived in America as well as in Italy. The Italian Pavilion was well represented with their displays of great art, sculpture, furniture, pottery, glassware, and rich fabrics.

Prohibition had a profound effect on The Hill from the early 1920s to WWII the area was somewhat identified as a "tough neighborhood" due to their involvement in the bootlegging trade. After Prohibition was repealed in 1933, restaurants, taverns, and nightclubs began to proliferate and flourish.

The St. Ambrose Catholic Church sits on the highest point of The Hill and continues to be the heart of the neighborhood. The fire hydrants are painted red, green, and white in honor of the Italian flag, and two of America's greatest baseball stars, Joe Garagiola and Yogi Berra, grew up on The Hill and across the street from each other. Even though many of its younger residents have moved away from the neighborhood, they still come back to St. Ambrose to baptize their children and to have wedding ceremonies. Some are returning to open businesses and to renovate the old shotgun houses that have stood there for over 100 years. The old timers are still there and the Italian way of life, the food shops, the restaurants, and the camaraderie, still exists to this day.

Rigazzi's

4945 Daggett Avenue, St. Louis

Within a 50-square-block area in south St. Louis is one of the city's great ethnic neighborhoods, The Hill, and its oldest restaurant, Rigazzi's, which has been a staple there for more than 50 years.

The history of Rigazzi's began in 1957 when Louis Aiazzi met John Riganti while they were both working at Ruggeri's, a restaurant on The Hill. Almost 30 years before, Louis Aiazzi's family had emigrated from Casteletto, a small town near Milan in Northern Italy, to the United States. The two men became friends and partners, combined their last names, and opened Rigazzi's. In 1961, Louis bought John's interest in the restaurant.

The restaurant soon became a favorite in the neighborhood and, at one point, Rigazzi's sold more Budweiser than any restaurant or bar in St. Louis. To show their appreciation, the Anheuser-Busch Brewery would bring their famed Clydesdale horses to the front of the restaurant for the patrons to enjoy.

In 2000, a devastating fire destroyed the interior of the restaurant. Luckily, the structure survived and eight months later the restaurant reopened under the stewardship of Louis's son, Mark Aiazzi and his wife, Joan, who still serve their famed frozen fishbowl — a giant 32-ounce frosty schooner of beer.

(courtesy of Rigazzi's)

Rigazzi's Chicken Giambetti

4 fresh sage leaves
12 medium shrimp, shelled and rinsed
6 tablespoons butter or margarine
1 cup diced pancetta (Italian bacon)
2 cups sliced mushrooms
Juice of 2 limes
6 tablespoons chopped garlic
4 tablespoons grated Parmesan cheese
2 grilled boneless, skinless chicken breasts (about ½ pound total)

Finely chop 2 of the fresh sage leaves. Set aside. Boil the shrimp until just opaque, about 8 minutes. Let cool until they are easy to handle, and dice.

In a saucepan, melt the butter over medium heat. Add the cooked and diced shrimp, pancetta, mushrooms, chopped sage, and garlic and sauté until the mushrooms begin to soften. Stir in the lime juice. When the sauce comes to simmer, stir in the Parmesan cheese.

To serve, place the grilled chicken breasts on individual plates and top with the sauce. Garnish each with a remaining whole sage leaf. Serve with Italian bread and a green salad tossed with Italian dressing. (At Rigazzi's, hearts of romaine lettuce is the preferred green, topped with their own house dressing.)

Serves 2

Louis Aiazzi, Martin Columbo, and John Riganti with the Budweiser Clydesdales, circa 1958 (courtesy of Joan Aiazzi)

(courtesy of Rigazzi's)

Lou Aiazzi's parent's wedding picture (courtesy of Rigazzi's)

Charlie Gitto's

5226 Shaw Avenue, St. Louis

Being a skilled coppersmith from Sicily came in handy when Salvatore Russo and his wife, Nunzia, immigrated to the United States and then to St. Louis's Little Italy community in the early 1900s. Along with his legitimate copper projects, Salvatore crafted the copper stills that would be used for making whiskey during Prohibition. It was a lucrative business, for sure, and when he died, Nunzia continued to make prohibited liquor and sold it from the basement of her home. Federal agents didn't take kindly to her entrepreneurial spirit, and promptly sent her off to jail.

Nunzia and Salvatore's daughter, Anna, married a local Italian American boy, Charlie Gitto. After a series of odd jobs, the couple opened Gitto's Pizza. The pizzeria was short lived, but Charlie went on to become a maitre'd at various fine restaurants in St. Louis. It was at Angelo's on The Hill, that Charlie felt most comfortable, and his family became close friends with Angelo's family.

Charlie's son, Charlie Jr., always loved Angelo's and hoped that one day he would be able to make it his own. Besides wanting to own the restaurant, Charlie Jr. also dreamed of being a professional baseball player. When the beloved Angelo passed away, his family wanted Charlie Jr. to take over the restaurant, so in 1981 Angelo's became Charlie Gitto's "On the Hill." Along with his mother, Anna, and his wife, Paula, they continue to feature both Northern and Southern dishes, as well as favorite American foods, which means you will not only find traditional dishes, but oysters and BBQ ribs. Their signature dish, Toasted Ravioli, was accidentally invented when a cook dropped some ravioli into some bread crumbs and fried them. It was an instant hit and Charlie Gitto's on The Hill has been a legend ever since.

(courtesy of Charlie Gitto's)

Charlie Gitto's Toasted Ravioli

Dough
3½ cups all-purpose flour
3 eggs
3 tablespoons corn oil
½ cup water
½ teaspoon salt

Meat filling
½ pound beef, cubed
½ pound veal, cubed
½ cup chopped onion
½ cup chopped celery
½ cup chopped carrots
Salt and pepper
1½ cups cooked, chopped spinach
4 eggs
4 ounces Parmesan, grated (1 cup)

Breading
4 eggs, beaten
2 cups milk
4 cups seasoned bread crumbs

Neutral-flavored oil, such as corn oil, for deep-frying
Grated Parmesan, for garnish
Tomato sauce, heated, for serving

Special equipment: ravioli cutter

Preheat the oven to 350°F.

To make the meat filling: Combine the beef, veal, onion, celery, carrots, salt, and pepper in a roasting pan and roast until cooked through, about 1 hour.

Saint Louis, circa 1874 (courtesy of Parsons & Atwater. A.G. Edwards, Co., St. Louis, MO)

While the filling is roasting, make the dough. Place all of the ingredients for the dough in a large mixing bowl. Using your hands or a stand mixer with a dough hook, mix the ingredients until they come together to form a dough. Turn the dough out onto a floured surface, and knead until smooth and elastic, about 10 to 15 minutes. Wrap in plastic wrap and set aside.

When the filling is done, remove from the oven and let cool. Add the spinach and then finely grind the ingredients in a meat grinder. (**Note:** If you do not have a meat grinder, grind the filling as finely as you can in a food processor and then continue mincing it by hand until the mixture is as close to the texture of ground meat as possible.) Add the eggs and cheese, and mix well, to create a pastelike texture.

Using a rolling pin, roll out the dough on a floured surface until very thin, about ⅛ of an inch. Using a spatula, spread a thin layer of the filling on half of one side of the dough. Fold the dough end over the filling side of the dough and score the ravioli with a paring knife to shape approximately

1-inch semi-circles. Then cut the ravioli out using a ravioli cutter, making sure the ends are sealed by pressing the edges. Freeze until hard.

To bread the ravioli: Make an egg wash by mixing together the eggs and the milk. Dip the ravioli in the wash, and then dip in the seasoned bread crumbs. The ravioli can be fried now or frozen for later use.

To fry the ravioli, pour 5 to 6 inches of oil into a deep-fryer or a deep saucepan and heat to 350°F. Fry the ravioli until golden brown. Serve hot with freshly grated Parmesan sprinkled on top and heated tomato sauce on the side.

Makes approximately 100 ravioli

"He who drinks wine before eating, can already
see the doctor from his window."
Italian proverb

New Orleans, Louisiana's French Quarter

Immigrants of French descent are not the only people who made the French Quarter their home. After 1850, when the first major wave of immigrants came to the United States, the French Quarter, in New Orleans Louisiana, also became the heart of the city's Italian American community. The area, known as "Little Palermo," claims to be the oldest, and at one time the largest, Italian neighborhood in the United States. It began when the immigrants, who came directly from Sicily on a 30-day passage, disembarked in New Orleans.

The climate and agriculture around New Orleans was similar to that in their native country, so the immigrants, most of whom had been farmers, were fortunate to find jobs on the many plantations that existed in Louisiana. Due to the language problem, the Italians were only able to earn fifty cents a day as opposed to one dollar a day for white workers and seventy-five cents a day for the black workers.

Although many went to work outside the city as farmers, some immigrants remained in the city, often working in food-related industries. Eventually, Italians in Louisiana would dominate the food industry, operating or working in everything from push carts and grocery stores to restaurants and food-processing plants. In 1940, before WWII, there were 642 Italian grocery stores in New Orleans, as those who did not go into farming

Opposite page: Caring for their own, the Unione Italiana of New Orleans collected food to make Christmas food baskets for the less fortunate members of the Italian community, circa 1935
(courtesy of American Italian Museum and Research Library and Salvatore J. Serio)

Picking strawberries at a local farm that was established to employ immigrant Italians, circa 1908 (courtesy of courtesy of American Italian Museum and Research Library and Salvatore J. Serio).

went into the grocery business, employing many of their family members and giving them a livelihood. It is said that the plantation workers would work all day, then sell fruit and vegetables by night — if they were lucky enough to acquire produce that "had fallen off of the truck." Long hours meant nothing and these immigrant Italians worked very hard as fruit sellers, bakers, and shoemakers to make a living for their families.

Traditional Italian celebrations and festivals were and still are an important part of family life and the Feast of St. Joseph remains one of the most significant. Centuries ago, a severe famine occurred in Sicily and many appealed to the "family protector," St. Joseph, to end the suffering. When this occurred, the townspeople, out of gratitude, prepared an altar with all of the foods they had harvested. When the Sicilians immigrated to New Orleans, they brought this tradition with them. Every year, on March 19th, altars are laid with all manner of candles, flowers, and food, including breads of all symbolic shapes, a variety of fish (meat is not permitted as this feast occurs during Lent), and many other gustatory delights, such as stuffed artichokes, pasta, fig cookies, and "lucky" fava beans, which are thought to be blessed. The fava bean was fodder for the cattle in Sicily but, during the famine, it was all the people had to eat to survive. Today it's believed that if you keep fava beans in your pantry, you will never go hungry. Another tradition holds that if bread is thrown outside the home during a storm, the inhabitants inside will be protected. During the Feast of St. Joseph, the children are allowed to eat before the adults and it is customary to give food to the needy on this holiday.

The fruit-import business was another major way that Italian Americans contributed to — and gained a livelihood in — the food industry. It became a big business in New Orleans, with oranges imported from the South and bananas imported from Honduras.

Market day in Independence, Louisiana, a thriving Italian community, circa 1904 (courtesy of courtesy of American Italian Museum and Research Library and Salvatore J. Serio)

It was another visionary family, the Vaccaro brothers, Joseph, Lucca, and Felix, that, in 1899, founded what would one day become the United Fruit Company, importing bananas to the United States.

The story of the Italians impact on the New Orleans food scene would not be complete without mention of the famous Muffuletta sandwich. It was at the famed Central Grocery across from the French Market in the French Quarter that the Muffuletta, or "Muffa" as the locals call it, was created. Having any number of spellings, the Muffuletta has a questionable beginning with many laying claim to its origin. However, in 1906, Sicilian immigrant Salvatore Lupo, a grocer at the Central invented what is believed to be "one of the great sandwiches of the world." The Muffa consists of a 10-inch-round Sicilian bread (which, according to legend, cannot be duplicated anywhere else because of the area's high humidity and the New Orleans water); an olive salad consisting of olives, celery, cauliflower, carrots, and olive oil; and a thick layer of Genoa salami, Italian ham, mortadella, and provolone. Once assembled, the sandwich is allowed to marinate. The exact proportions of the olive salad are a closely guarded secret. This sandwich is indicative of this region and is just not the same when served in other parts of the United States.

The city of New Orleans is rich in the traditions of the Italians who have endured great hardships including floods and Hurricanes Katrina and Rita. But true to their roots, they are a strong and vibrant people who are intent on preserving their unique culture as they help their neighbors rebuild. They will continue to give the cuisine of New Orleans a special, flavorful twist (they might even add a little oregano to their gumbo).

Antoine's Restaurant

713 Rue Saint Louis, New Orleans

There is no doubt that New Orleans is one of the premier dining centers in the United States. And in New Orleans, Antoine's, with its stellar reputation, is the place to dine and to be seen. It is the spot where Oysters Rockefeller was invented and countless celebrities have dined, and it has the distinction of being the country's oldest family-run restaurant.

Surprisingly, it was an Italian who emigrated from France to the United States, Antoine Alciatore, who created the most celebrated French Creole eating establishment in the South.

After a disappointing two years in New York, the young Antoine set his sights on New Orleans. He began working in the kitchen of the St. Charles Hotel and soon after, in 1840, opened his own boarding house and restaurant. Within five years, his Pension Alciatore was a known destination.

Five years later, his fiancée joined him and they, along with her sister, established its reputation as a culinary landmark. By 1868, they had already outgrown their location and moved to Rue Saint Louis, where they remain to this day, and the Pension Alciatore became known as Antoine's Restaurant. Sadly, Antoine became ill and in 1874, when so many Italians were then making their way to the United States, he traveled back to his birthplace in France to live out his few remaining months, leaving his wife and family to carry on his legacy. His son, Jules, after apprenticing at the great restaurants of Paris, Strasburg, and Marseilles and in 1887 he returned to New Orleans as chef at the Pickwick Club. His mother summoned him to head Antoine's where he is credited with inventing the legendary dish, Oysters Rockefeller (with its signature green sauce), named not for the Rockefeller family, but for the richness of the sauce.

Jules married Althea Roy and, they had two children, Marie Louise and Roy Louis. It was Roy who headed Antoine's for almost 40 years, through the Depression, Prohibition and two World War II until his death in 1972. Marie Louise married

(courtesy of Antoine's Restaurant)

William Guste, and their sons, William Jr. and Roy, became fourth-generation restauranteurs. By 1975, Roy Jr., a fifth-generation family member, was at the helm, and he was followed by William's son Bernard ("Randy") Guste.

Countless celebrities from the Duke and Duchess of Windsor to Pope Paul II, as well as the elite of New Orleans society, have dined in one of the fifteen unique and historical dining rooms that house countless photographs and memorabilia. Each dining room is distinctive, recalling a different era in the life of Antoine's and New Orleans. Four of the rooms are re-named for the Mardi Gras Carnival, which has been the main attraction in New Orleans since it was officially started in 1873, thirty-three years after Antoine's first opened (when it was still known as Pension Alciatore). The Rex, Proteus, Hermes, and 12th Night Revelers were named for the Carnival krewes (the organizations that put on Mardi Gras). Other rooms are the Large Annex, the Roy Alciatore Room, the Maison Verte, the Japanese Room (which was closed for forty-three years after the bombing of Pearl Harbor), and the Mystery Room, which gained its name during, Prohibition when patrons went through the ladies room to a secret room and exited with a coffee cup full of liquor. When asked where the cup came from, the answer would be, "It's a mystery to me." And then there is the 1840 Room, the Veranda Room, the Art Gallery Room, and, of course, the renowned Wine Cellar, which holds 25,000 bottles of wine when fully stocked.

Antoine's is a bastion of rich and sumptuous food, including exquisite sauces, melt-in-your-mouth seafood, and the never-ending Pommes de terre soufflées. However, finding a table at this coveted restaurant, might be the real adventure!

Antoine's Shrimp Salad with Rémoulade Sauce

1 ½ pounds shrimp with shells

2 quarts water

2 teaspoons Zatarain's® Shrimp and Crab Boil

½ head lettuce, shredded

1 hard-boiled egg, chopped, for garnish

1 teaspoon chopped fresh Italian (flat-leaf) parsley, for garnish

Rémoulade Sauce

¾ cup ketchup

2 teaspoons horseradish

2 teaspoons Creole mustard

1 teaspoon Worcestershire

Tabasco sauce, to taste

1 teaspoon chopped green onion

Bring the water and Shrimp Crab and Boil seasoning to a boil in a stockpot. Add the shrimp and boil for 2½ minutes. Drain and let cool slightly. Peel the shrimp and set aside.

To make the Rémoulade Sauce: Combine all of the ingredients in a bowl and chill in the refrigerator.

To serve, divide the lettuce among four cold salad plates. Mix the shrimp and the Rémoulade Sauce together and spoon one-quarter of the mixture onto the bed of lettuce on each plate. Sprinkle with the egg and parsley.

Serves 4

(courtesy of Antoine's Restaurant)

Antoine's Pompano Pontchartrain

4 (4 to 8-ounce) pompano fillets (trout may be substituted)

3 tablespoons extra-virgin olive oil

1 teaspoon salt

1 teaspoon white pepper

Crabmeat Topping

6 ounces (1½ sticks) butter

½ tablespoon chopped green onion

12 ounces cooked jumbo lump crabmeat

Juice of 1 lemon

Salt and black pepper, to taste

For Garnish

1 lemon, cut into 4 wedges

Chopped fresh Italian (flat-leaf) parsley

Preheat a grill or flat griddle. Sprinkle the fillets with the oil, salt and white pepper. Cook on the hot grill or griddle for 3 to 4 minutes on each side. Set aside in a low oven to keep warm.

To make the crabmeat topping: In a skillet, melt the butter over medium heat. Add the green onions and cook for 1 to 2 minutes. Add the crabmeat, lemon juice, salt, and pepper and stir to combine. Cook just long enough to heat crabmeat through.

To serve, divide the fish fillets among four plates. Place ¾ cup of the crabmeat topping on each serving of fish. Garnish each plate with a wedge of lemon and a sprinkling of chopped parsley.

Serves 4

Antoine's Caramel Custard

Caramel Sauce

¾ cup sugar

¾ cup water

Custard

4 eggs

¾ cup sugar

1 teaspoon pure vanilla extract

Pinch of salt

1 pint half-and-half (2 cups)

Preheat the oven to 340°F.

To make the caramel sauce: Combine the sugar and water in a small saucepan.

Cook over medium-high heat for 10 minutes, stirring continuously for the first 5 minutes, and stirring and checking every 2 minutes thereafter, until light brown (caramelized). Pour the syrup into bottom of four 6-ounce custard cups.

To make the custard: Whisk together the eggs, sugar, vanilla, and salt in a large bowl. Heat the half-and-half (do not boil). Slowly pour the cream into the egg mixture while continuously whisking until creamy. Pour the custard into the prepared cups, then place cups in a pan of heated water. Bake for approximately 1 hour (when done, the centers will hold firm when shaken). Chill in refrigerator before serving.

To serve, loosen custard edges with a small knife, turn out onto a cold plate.

Garnish with a mint leaf, powdered sugar, and strawberries.

Serves 4

Map of New Orleans circa 1885 (courtesy of Historic New Orleans Collection, New Orleans, L.A.)

"When baking, follow directions, when cooking, go by your own taste."
Italian proverb

San Francisco's North Beach

The discovery of gold in 1848 at Sutter's Mill in Coloma, California, along the banks of the South Fork of the American River, changed the United States forever. Between 1849 and 1852, the population of California spiked from 90,000 to 220,000 and, by 1855, the population reached 300,000, gold seekers, immigrants, and merchants.

News of the riches in the gold mines spurred Italians from Liguria and Tuscany to emigrate from their homeland in search of wealth that few of the immigrants would ever realize. Finding the life of a gold prospector difficult and not often rewarding, the Italian men, who mostly came to the United States alone to make their fortunes, leaving their families behind in Italy, found employment in familiar trades such as fishing, craft trades, small businesses, and agriculture.

Many gold-seeking (and gold-bust) immigrants ended up in San Francisco. Before the gold rush, the city of San Francisco was a small settlement with its growth centered in its port, but the effects of the gold rush would be the catalyst for a legendary building boom that included construction of new buildings, roads, churches, and most importantly, the railroads throughout the state — all of which would lead to California's statehood in 1850. By the beginning of the twentieth century, members of San Francisco's prosperous and stable Italian community founded banks, newspapers, mutual aid societies, theaters,

Opposite page: Opening day at the Caffé Trieste (courtesy of Caffé Trieste)

A banquet during the Panama-Pacific Exposition at the Fior d'Italia celebrating the first mayor of Rome after Italian reunification, circa 1915 (courtesy of Fior d'Italia)

schools, churches, clubs, and a cemetery. The dream of returning to Italy had long disappeared.

Part of the famed Barbary Coast, North Beach — the name which now refers to the Italian neighborhood — is steeped in history and tradition. Bordered by Chinatown and Fisherman's Wharf with Telegraph Hill and Coit Tower on the east, and Russian Hill to the west, the Italian quarter of North Beach has weathered many decades of decay as well as revitalization through gentrification. The devastating earthquake and fire that occurred on April 18, 1906 was considered a catastrophic act of God, but in keeping with the Italian spirit, many thousands of gallons of their prized wine were used to put out the flames in their neighborhoods. In the 1950s and '60s, it was a gritty working-class neighborhood that attracted the likes of such famed poets as Jack Kerouac and Allen Ginsberg, and it was also the birthplace of the legendary baseball player, Joe DiMaggio, who at one point lived in this neighborhood with his wife, Marilyn Monroe.

The Italian population has made a huge impact on the flavor and culture of San Francisco. From music to food, banking to fishing, and politics to entertainment, the Italian influence is ever present. And as is the case with all Italian communities in the United States, Italian-aid societies were formed, and in San Franciso more than 100 societies were started that are present to this day, catering to all manner of needs of the Italian population. The climate in San Francisco was so similar to the sunny cities that line the Mediterranean Sea that the Italian immigrants immediately felt at home and set out to work as vintners, fishermen, and fruit growers as they had done in their homeland. Today, North Beach is a lively and vital tourist destination, filled with colorful restaurants, cafés, and bakeries. It is now definitely worthy of its illustrious history.

writing his screenplay for *The Godfather* while others stop by to enjoy a special coffee or to listen to the guitar and mandolin or to hear the melodic voices that waft through the air like the smell of the espresso they so love.

Caffé Trieste Caffé Fantasia

2 tablespoons grated semi-sweet chocolate
½ cup extra-rich milk (see note)
Freshly brewed shot of espresso
1½ ounces Torani orgeat (almond) syrup
3 tablespoons fresh whipped cream
Ground cinnamon, for garnish

In a 10-ounce mug, add the semi-sweet chocolate. Add the milk and, with the steam-pipe of an espresso machine or a milk steamer, heat and froth milk in the normal manner. Make sure to keep the steamer tip at the bottom of the mug long enough to thoroughly mix the chocolate and the milk.

Add the shot of espresso and the orgeat syrup, and thoroughly mix. Then add enough of the remaining steamed milk to fill the mug to within three-quarters of an inch from the top. Top with the whipped cream and a sprinkling of cinnamon.

Note: The baristas at Caffé Trieste use milk from dairy farms in Northern California, along the coast. They say it is richer than whole milk but less rich than half-and-half. If you don't have access to especially rich whole milk, simply add some half-and-half to regular whole milk.

Serves 1

"Those who sleep don't catch any fish."
Italian proverb

San Diego, California's Little Italy

In keeping with the tradition of seeking a better life, some Italian immigrants who landed at Ellis Island in New York City made their way west to San Francisco, the gold rush boom town. However, after the 1906 earthquake, many Italian families decided that it might be safer to move further south. San Diego was the ideal spot for them as the weather closely resembled that of their homes of Genoa, Naples, or Sicily. And since most of the Italians were fishermen by trade the coastal setting was perfect for them.

At first, the catch in the waters off the coast of San Diego was mackerel and sardines. It was when tuna began to appear that the industry exploded. By 1910, the first tuna cannery opened, drawing even more Italians, as well as Portuguese, and by 1930 there were more than 6,000 Italian families living in what became their Little Italy — an area consisting of just a few blocks on India Street close to the downtown and very close to the ocean. At that time, 90 percent of all the tuna was canned on the West Coast, and, in this coastal Little Italy, where 75 percent of all the families earned their living from fishing, their work had a direct influence on what they would eat. The baking of bread for the fishing trips, a community effort, was done by the wives of the fisherman. If the

Opposite page (courtesy of Chris Gomez, San Diego Little Italy Association)

(courtesy of Joanne DiBona)

catch was good that day, the brick ovens were fired up, the garlic was sautéed, the wine poured, and a feast would be enjoyed by all.

In this closely knit community, where the lives of so many families were intertwined, the children probably thought that Little Italy was one big family, and that everyone was a relative. But, as with so many communities, change happens. Many of the men went off to fight in WWII, and during that time the government seized their tuna boats for use in the South Pacific. After the war, the fish imported from Japan undercut their prices and many fishermen were forced to find other means of support. One by one, canneries began to close and then, as if things couldn't get any worse, in 1962, a 2½-mile section of Interstate 5 was built right through San Diego's Little Italy community, cutting it in half! Many who had built their lives there were forced to relocate, with a devastating effect on families, friends, and livelihoods.

What held the community together through this upheaval was Our Lady of the Rosary Roman Catholic Church, which was then and is today the mainstay of the Italian American community in San Diego. From christenings to funerals, it was the core that would bring friends and relatives together for Sunday masses, spaghetti suppers, newsletters, street processions, and carnivals. It was that way when it was built in 1925 and it still remains so today.

But rather than vanishing, this community is having a great rebirth. Little Italy today represents downtown San Diego's oldest continuous neighborhood business district. The construction of apartments and mixed-use developments has skyrocketed. In October 1994, Little Italy in San Diego began to experience a rebirth. Restaurants, cafes —and street life have returned to this community with a flourish. India Street was reopened with a small festa (Italian festival), which has now grown into the largest, single-day

Portugese and Italian fishing boats in San Diego Bay, circa 1930 (courtesy of The Waterfront Bar and Grill)

Italian festa west of the Mississippi. The scent of sautéed garlic and fresh bread wafts along India Street and the Italian community, and people from all over come to eat and celebrate the memory of what the Italian community and the fishermen left to San Diego. In the salt air from the nearby ocean, you can still catch a whiff of tomato sauce simmering and fish frying. The fish may no longer be caught but the spirit of community still lingers in the warm greetings you'll find here and the flavors that will take you back to the Italy you love.

Filippi's Pizza Grotto

1747 India Street, San Diego

(courtesy of Filippi's Pizza Grotto)

The DePhilippis family moved to California from the Fordham section of the Bronx when a friend of theirs told them that the East Coast winters were so cold that it would be too expensive to clothe their seven children. Madeleine had immigrated to the U.S. from France in 1922, the same year her future husband, Vincent DePhilippis emigrated from Italy. They married in 1925 and after taking their friend's advice, headed west to the warmth of California.

In 1950, Madeleine and Vincent DePhilippis arrived in Los Angeles with their seven children and, after less than a year, the family relocated to San Diego, where Vincent was to operate the Di Rocco Macaroni factory. When the macaroni factory job didn't work out, and after another disappointing

Vincent DePhilippis, circa 1955 (courtesy of Filippi's Pizza Grotto and Danny Moceri)

job at an airplane factory, Vincent purchased a former bar that had been in San Diego since 1908 and was owned by a local Italian immigrant, John Oliato. Before that, a butcher shop had been in the same spot. The DePhilippis' full Italian grocery store now took its place. Vincent would travel to Los Angeles to pick up products and very soon established trust and respect from the Italian community.

While patrons and the local fisherman would wait for their grocery order to be filled, they would be served Italian sandwiches and small pizzas with beefy meatballs and homemade sausage that was prepared in the back of the store. In time, a restaurant evolved, providing a needed place for the fishermen to congregate and eat and drink with one another. The wine bottles that still hang from the ceiling harken back to the days when the workers, after a long day at sea, would come to socialize and drink wine. The fishermen wanted the bottles hung so that they would be able to keep track of the amount of wine they consumed.

Though San Diego's freeway building projects, which were completed in 1962, took a huge toll on the Little Italy community in San Diego — as grandson and now general manager, Danny Moceri, tells it, "Between Elliot Ness and the I-5 freeway, they got rid of a lot of Italians" — the DePhilippis family not only remained but they expanded their business. Today, you will always find a family member to serve you in their little empire of twelve family-owned restaurants.

Madeleine DePhilippis, circa 1960 (courtesy of Filippi's Pizza Grotto and Danny Moceri)

(courtesy of Filippi's Pizza Grotto)

Filippi's Pizza Grotto Shrimp Filippi

2 tablespoons extra-virgin olive oil

1 tablespoon chopped garlic

1½ cups chopped green onions

1 cup sliced mushrooms

½ lemon, cut into wedges

1 cup jumbo bay shrimp

¾ cup cooking Marsala wine

2 tablespoons butter, room temperature

Pinch of salt and black pepper

Pinch of oregano

8 ounces dried linguini pasta

Cook the pasta in a large pot of boiling salted water according to package directions. Drain well.

In a skillet, heat the oil over low heat. Add the garlic, onions, and mushrooms and cook for approximately 2 minutes, until softened. Add the shrimp and cook for 2 minutes. Increase the heat to high and add the Marsala wine and cook for 1 minute. Add the lemon wedges and cook for 1 minute or less. Add the butter and season with the salt, pepper, and oregano.

To serve, divide the pasta between two plates. Top with the shrimp and sauce.

Serves 2

(courtesy of Joanne DiBona)

Solunto Baking Co.

1643 India Street, San Diego

Bread making comes from the heart and, at Solunto's, it comes from the heart of Mario Cefalu, a kind and gentle man who was the founder of the Solunto Baking Company. Solunto Bakery, which has become a landmark, bakes breads the way they have been made for centuries in Italy. The son of a Sicilian importer-exporter of olive oils and cheeses, Mario Cefalu emmigrated from Sicily to Boston in 1946, but didn't see a future for himself there. He then moved to the Bensonhurst section of Brooklyn and remained there for nineteen years, moving on to the Bay Ridge area for a short time. Feeling that New York was too competitive, he vacationed in San Diego and, after a short stint in Santa Barbara and Los Angeles, he settled in San Diego in 1968 and established his baking empire there. In the process, he became a well-respected figure in the San Diego Little Italy community.

At the bakery, Mario's son Dominick still bakes filone — a large, tube-shaped loaf, shorter than a baguette, made with naturally soured dough that forms a nice golden-brown crust when baked. He also makes Italian baguettes, boules, and seeded rolls, all of which are baked the old-fashioned way — al marmo — meaning, a bit chewier. An electric mixer mixes the dough, and the one-pound pieces are weighed on an antique balance scale. The loaves are then shaped and put into a wooden proofing box to rise. At the proper moment, the loaves are slid into the brick oven using a long wooden peel (as the wooden spatula is called).

No sugar, additives, or preservatives are used and no animal fat or shortenings are added. Homemade pizza, sausages, and arancini — fried rice balls coated with breadcrumbs and filled with a meat ragu — are served at Solunto, but it is really the bread that most customers are after. Way before jet planes even landed in San Diego, it is said that Frank Sinatra used to order bread from Solunto to

Founder of Solunto, Mario Cefalu, circa 1968 (courtesy of Solunto Baking Co.)

be sent to his home in Palm Springs. As weather, temperature, and humidity all make a difference in bread making, the bakers at Solunto taste the fermentation in the yeast to make sure each batch of loaves is perfect. And then they get to see the satisfaction on the faces of their customers.

Solunto's Sicilian Arancino

Risotto

2 tablespoons extra-virgin olive oil

1 medium onion, chopped

2 cups uncooked Arborio rice

6 cups chicken broth

1 teaspoon saffron

2 eggs, beaten

1 cup grated Parmigiano-Reggiano cheese (about 4 ounces)

Meat Ragu

2 tablespoons extra-virgin olive oil

1 medium onion, chopped

3 sweet Italian sausages, casings removed,
 or 1 pound ground beef

1 (28-ounce) can crushed Italian plum tomatoes

Salt, to taste

½ teaspoon red pepper flakes (optional)

2 cups frozen peas

6 fresh basil leaves, chopped

Breading

2 eggs

2 to 3 cups breadcrumbs

Neutral-flavored oil (vegetable or canola), for deep-frying

To make the risotto: Heat the olive oil in a medium saucepan over medium heat. Add the onion and cook until soft. Add the rice all at once and stir to coat well.

Add the broth, ½ cup at a time, stirring the rice until the broth has been absorbed between each addition. Once the risotto is cooked and creamy, remove from the heat.

Transfer the risotto to a large bowl to cool. Add the saffron, beaten eggs, and grated Parmigiano cheese to the cooled rice and mix well. Refrigerate until ready to use. Cold risotto is easier to handle when shaping the arancino.

To make the ragu: In a medium-sized saucepan, heat the olive oil over medium-high heat. Add the onion and cook until soft. Add the sausage meat or ground beef.

Break up the meat with a wooden spoon and cook until the meat is no longer pink.

Add the crushed tomatoes, salt, and red pepper flakes, if using. Cook for about 30 minutes and then add the peas.

Simmer the sauce on low heat for another 30 minutes, or until it has thickened. Remove from the heat and let cool.

To form the arancino: Beat the eggs in a medium bowl. Place the breadcrumbs on a large plate. Line a large tray with paper towels.

Remove the risotto from the refrigerator. Place 1 cup of the rice in the palm of your hand and shape into a cup. Place 1 tablespoon of the meat ragu in the cup and close the rice over the ragu, pinching the ends together, to form a sealed round ball. Roll the arancino in the beaten eggs and then in the breadcrumbs. Set on the prepared tray. Continue to make the arancino using this method until all the risotto and ragu has been used. Refrigerate 30 minutes.

Line another tray with paper towels. Heat 3 to 4 inches of the neutral-flavored oil in a deep saucepan or deep-fryer to 375°F. Fry the arancino no more than three at a time until golden brown. Remove the arancino with a slotted spoon and place on the second tray lined with paper towels to drain. Arrange on a platter and serve hot or at room temperature.

Serves 5 to 6

Trattoria Fantastica

1735 India Street, San Diego

Although relatively new to the community of Little Italy, the Busalacchi family has transformed the restaurant scene in San Diego with their generations-old Southern Italian peasant-food dishes.

It began when Pietro Busalacchi emigrated from Palermo, Sicily in 1966. Speaking no English, he came to San Diego as a tuna fisherman. But by that time, the mayor of San Diego was concerned about the fishing nets harming the porpoises that were happily swimming off the coast of San Diego. The fishing industry, which was already having difficulty competing with the lower-priced fish from Japan, began to falter.

It was Pietro's son, Joe, one of seven children, who became interested in the restaurant business by visiting his father's homeland in Sicily and learning the restaurant trade. Working with the tuna fleet, and along with the inspiration of his grandmother (who instilled in him the love of food and its proper preparation), he became a chef aboard a tuna boat for five years.

1735 India Street San Diego CA 92101 (619) 234-1735
Little Italy   trattoriafantas.signonsandiego.com

(courtesy of Trattoria Fantastica)

By the time the I-5 freeway cut through San Diego's Little Italy, most of its residents had scattered and the neighborhood was no longer the quaint place it once was. But, by the early 1990s, there was a rebirth and redevelopment of the Little Italy community. Joe Busalacchi was in the right place at the right time, and took the opportunity to amass a group of the best restaurants in San Diego and, most importantly, Little Italy. Some of his most popular dishes include Pasta with Broccoli, Sausages with Capers and Olives, his Cassata Siciliana, a traditional sweet from Palermo made with sponge cake, marzipan, ricotta, and fruit — and the cannolis, of course, are his grandmother's prized recipe.

Although Joe believes that Americans do not always eat healthily, he pays strict attention to the preparation of the dishes on his menu by using the freshest of ingredients as well as implementing slow and exacting presentation. Most nights, he plays host to entertainment and sports celebrities like Anderson Cooper, Jerry Lewis, Joe Pesci, Frankie Avalon, Mike Piazza, Tommy Lasorda and Frankie Laine — so, he must be doing something right!

(courtesy of Trattoria Fantastica)

Trattoria Fantastica's Penne Contadina

Neutral-flavored oil, for deep-frying

¼ cup julienned eggplant strips

3 tablespoons extra-virgin olive oil

2 tablespoons chopped garlic

1 medium zucchini, finely chopped

¾ cup quartered artichoke hearts (water packed), drained

1 cup sliced mushrooms

1 cup chopped fresh tomatoes

1 pound dried penne pasta

3 tablespoons crumbled gorgonzola cheese

Salt and black pepper, to taste

3 tablespoons chopped fresh basil leaves, for garnish

In a deep-sided saucepan or small deep-fryer, heat 3 to 4 inches of oil to 375°F. Fry the eggplant strips until crisp, about 3 to 4 minutes. Drain well on paper towels.

Bring a large pot of salted water to a boil.

In a skillet, heat the oil over medium-low heat. Add the garlic and sauté until golden. Add zucchini, artichokes, mushrooms, and tomatoes. Simmer for 5 minutes over low heat.

While the sauce is simmering, cook the pasta in the salted boiling water until al dente. Drain well.

Add the gorgonzola cheese, salt, and pepper to the skillet with the vegetables, and mix well. When the cheese has melted, pour the mixture over the pasta. Garnish with the eggplant strips and chopped basil.

Serves 4

Trattoria Fantastica's Pasta Palermitana

2 tablespoons garlic

1 pound sweet or hot Italian bulk sausage or link sausage with casings removed

3 tablespoons extra-virgin olive oil

½ tablespoon hot pepper flakes

½ tablespoon capers

2 tablespoons coarsely chopped green olives

3 cups canned diced tomatoes with juice (about two 14.5-ounce cans)

1 pound dried rigatoni

3 tablespoons chopped fresh Italian (flat-leaf) parsley, for garnish

Bring a large pot of salted water to a boil.

In a large skillet, heat the oil over medium heat. Brown the garlic and sausage in the hot oil. Add the remaining ingredients, except the parsley. Simmer for 10 minutes over medium-low heat.

While the sauce is simmering, cook the pasta in the boiling salted water until al dente. Drain well and add to the sauce. Toss the pasta and sauce together until well combined. Transfer to a serving platter and garnish with the chopped parsley.

Serves 4

Painting of Italian tuna fishermen in San Diego (courtesy of Joanne DiBona)

Mona Lisa Italian Restaurant and Deli

2061 India Street, San Diego

When Stefano Brunetto emigrated from Aspra, Sicily to the United States in 1949, he left behind a life of struggle. The Brunetto family were fish peddlers and would salt and can anchovies in their home. Upon immigrating, Stefano worked on the tuna boats while trying to establish himself in the restaurant business. While struggling in the 1950s and '60s, he returned to tuna fishing until that industry collapsed, but, by that time, he and his family had accomplished the American Dream by establishing themselves in a thriving and successful restaurant business.

Now, three generations of the Brunettos serve the likes of actors Timothy Hutton and Lorenzo Lamas, and sports celebrities Dan Fouts and Tommy Lasorda. The Mona Lisa boasts an extensive menu serving copious portions of lasagna and Veal alla Mona Lisa, coupled with a market deli in the front of the restaurant, rivaling any Italian market anywhere.

Mona Lisa Pasta Primavera

4 ounces (1 stick) butter

1½ teaspoons chopped garlic

1 quart (4 cups) heavy cream

1 pound dried rotini pasta

2 large carrots (about ½ pound), peeled and julienned

2 broccoli spears, florets separated and stems peeled
  and cut into ½-inch rounds

½ head of cauliflower, cut into florets

1 pound Parmesan cheese, grated

4 ounces Romano cheese, grated

Chopped fresh Italian (flat-leaf) parsley, for garnish

Bring a large pot of salted water to a boil. Parboil the vegetables for 2 to 3 minutes. Remove with a strainer or slotted spoon and plunge into a bowl of ice water to

Mona Lisa

ITALIAN RESTAURANT & DELI

JOHN BRUNETTO
OWNER/MANAGER
2061 INDIA STREET, SAN DIEGO, CA 92101

(619) 234-4893

(courtesy of Mona Lisa Italian Restaurant and Deli)

stop cooking. Drain and set aside. (Do not discard the parboiling water.)

In a large skillet, melt the butter over medium-high heat. Add the garlic and sauté until soft. Add the cream and bring to a simmer over low heat.

Bring the pot of salted water to a boil again and add the rotini. Cook until al dente. Drain well and add to the cream mixture along with the vegetables and Parmesan. Over low heat, toss the pasta until it is completely coated with the cream and the vegetables are re-heated and mixed in. Top with the Romano cheese and parsley.

Note: Any combination of leftover vegetables can be used for primavera. The above combination is one of Mona Lisa's favorites for Primavera, but they stress than any vegetables can be used. This pasta dish is a great way to use up leftover vegetables!

Serves 7 to 8

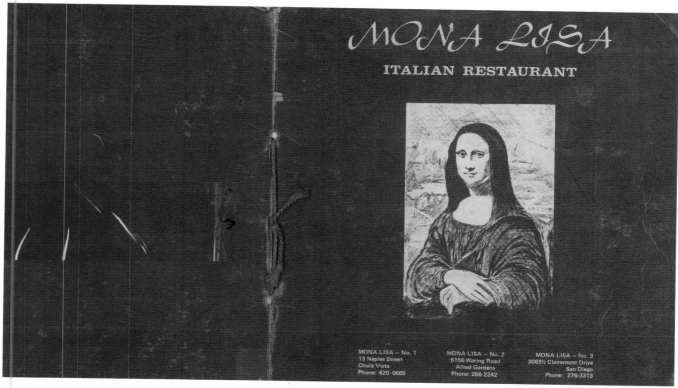

MONA LISA
ITALIAN RESTAURANT

MONA LISA — No. 1
13 Naples Street
Chula Vista
Phone: 420-0665

MONA LISA — No. 2
5156 Waring Road
Allied Gardens
Phone: 286-2242

MONA LISA — No. 3
3083½ Clairemont Drive
San Diego
Phone: 276-3313

A La Carte
Pizza

All Our Pizzas Are Made With Tomato and Mozzarella Cheese

HAM	$4.00
MOZZARELLA CHEESE	3.30
PROVOLONE CHEESE	4.00
ANCHOVIES	4.00
PEPPERONI	4.00
ITALIAN SAUSAGE	4.00
A. MUSHROOMS AND SAUSAGE	4.90
B. MUSHROOMS AND PEPPERONI	4.90
MUSHROOMS	4.30
ITALIAN SAUSAGE, PEPPERONI, MUSHROOMS, ANCHOVIES AND ONIONS	5.50
SAUSAGE AND PEPPERONI	4.90
HAMBURGER	~~2.95~~ 4.00
BLACK OLIVE	4.30
GREEN PEPPER	4.00

SMALL ANTIPASTO . . . . . $ .95   ANTIPASTO $2.40

MINESTRONE SOUP . . . . Cup $ .80 / Bowl $1.00

Spaghetti, Ravioli & Lasagna

Dishes Below Served With Roll and Butter / Meat Balls or Italian Sausage $.75 Extra

SPAGHETTI	Half Order – $1.75	Full Order – $2.75
RAVIOLI	Half Order – $1.95	Full Order – $2.95
HALF and HALF (Spaghetti & Ravioli)		$2.95
LASAGNA IMBOTTITA (Stuffed Noodles Italian Style) *half order $1.85*		$3.25
MANICOTTI (Large Macaroni Shell Stuffed With Cheese)		$3.00
CANNELLONI (Large Macaroni Shell Stuffed With Meat)		$3.00

Sandwiches

HAM	$1.60	TORPEDO $1.40
SALAMI	1.50	SAUSAGE 1.70
MEAT BALLS	1.70	HAM AND CHEESE 1.70

GARLIC BREAD . . . . . $ .80

— NO SUBSTITUTES PLEASE —

— FOOD TO GO — ($.10 for container)

Dinners
—INCLUDES—
Salad ● Coffee ● Bread & Butter
ENTREE

Meat Balls or Italian Sausage — $.75 Extra

SPAGHETTI WITH MEAT SAUCE	$3.60
RAVIOLI WITH MEAT SAUCE	3.80
HALF AND HALF	3.80
RIGATONI, SHELL, MUSTACCIOLI or LINGUINE	4.70
LASAGNA IMBOTTITA	4.10
MANICOTTI	4.00
CANNELLONI	4.00
GNOCCHI AL FORNO	4.00

Family Dinners

Antipasto Salad – Spaghetti & Meat Ball – Ravioli – Lasagna

Pizza – Roll & Butter – Coffee

For Two $10.50 — For Three $15.00 — For Four $20.00

Additional Persons $4.50 Each / Children 1/2 Price

Mona Lisa

*Invites You to Try Her Own
Selection House Wine*

RED – WHITE – ROSE

1/4 Litro $1.00 / 1/2 Litro $2.00 / Litro $3.65

Per Glass – $.50

Drinks and Desserts

CANNOLI	$ .75	BEER (On Tap)	$ .40
SPUMONI (Ice Cream)	.60	DARK BEER	.45
COFFEE	.35	BOTTLED BEER (Domestic)	.50 .65
MILK	.40	BOTTLED BEER (Imported)	1.00
SOFT DRINKS	.35	MICHELOB	.75
ICE TEA	.35		

Wine List

RED DINNER WINES

	½ Bottle	Full Bottle
1. Mountain Red Burgundy, Almadén	$1.75	$2.80
2. Pinot Noir, Almadén	$2.40	$3.70
3. Zinfandel, Almadén	$2.40	$3.70

— Imported Wines —

MATEUS ROSÉ	LANCERS ROSÉ
Large $4.50	Large $5.50
Small $2.75	Small $3.50

ROSÉ DINNER WINES

	½ Bottle	Full Bottle
5. Mountain Nectar Vin Rose, Almadén	$2.10	$3.50
6. Grenache Rose, Almadén	$2.10	$3.50

WHITE DINNER WINES

	½ Bottle	Full Bottle
7. Mountain White Chablis, Almadén	$1.90	$2.90
8. Mountain Rhine Chablis, Almadén	$1.90	$2.90

*Un Pranzo Senza Vino
E Come Una Giornata
Senza Sole*

The Waterfront Bar and Grill

2044 Kettner Blvd., San Diego

San Diego's Oldest Tavern

FOOD   COCKTAILS

WATERFRONT
IN LITTLE ITALY
2044 KETTNER BLVD. (619) 232-9656
BILLY BONNET

(courtesy of The Waterfront Bar and Grill)

The Waterfront Bar and Grill has been in operation since before Prohibition (and most likely it operated unofficially during that period as a speakeasy). "Officially," it was the first bar to open in San Diego after Prohibition and was owned by the grandson of Ulysses S. Grant. The Waterfront was a popular meeting place for the local Italian and Portuguese fishing fleets. They would come to drink and eat for less than a quarter, while mending their nets outside in front of the bar. The railroad tracks were directly behind the bar and below that was the San Diego Bay where all of the docks and the tuna canneries operated.

The Waterfront Bar and Grill used to be, as its name suggests, on the waterfront, but the construction of the I-5 freeway in the 1960s, split the community in half and landfill was added to make way for new streets and structures, which were built between the bar and the San Diego Bay. The view of the ocean is now blocked by these buildings and the landscape has changed forever.

Today, the Waterfront Bar and Grill specializes in "Italian-style" fish and chips and the best burgers in San Diego. The walls are so full of memorabilia that you don't know where to look first. It is also frequented by many local celebrities, but in the days of the speakeasy, it was Wyatt Earp, the legendary gunman of the Old West, who hung his hat at the Waterfront.

Waterfront Bar Italian-Style Deep-Fried Fish and Chips

1 pound fresh fish fillets (Pollack or any mild whitefish)
All-purpose flour, for dredging
1 egg, slightly beaten with 1 teaspoon water
1 cup Italian crumbs
Neutral-flavored oil, preferably canola, for frying

Cut the fish into 3-inch squares. Dip the fish pieces in flour, then the egg wash, and finally in the bread crumbs.

In a large skillet, heat ¼ to ½-inch of canola oil over medium-high heat. When the oil is 375°F (use a deep-fat or candy thermometer to read the temperature of the oil), shallow-fry the fish until golden brown, about 4 to 6 minutes on each side. Serve with tartar sauce, French fries or cottage fries, and coleslaw.

Serves 3

This neon sign marks the entrance to San Diego Little Italy (courtesy of Joanne DiBona)

(courtesy of The Sicilian Festival of San Diego)

San Diego, California's Little Italy | **215**

PART III
GLOSSARY
From Antipasto to Ziti

A

abbacchio: Spring lamb that is milk-fed not grass-fed

aceto: Vinegar

aceto balsamico: The best of all Italian vinegars. It is dark brown in color with a mellow, sweet flavor.

acciughe: Anchovies

affogare: To poach

aglio: Garlic

agnello: Lamb

agnolotti: Type of ravioli filled with meat, cheese, or spinach

anguilla: Eel

al dente: The point at which pasta is perfectly cooked — "to the tooth"

amaretti: An Italian almond macaroon cookie flavored with bitter almonds

amaretto: Sweet almond-flavored liqueur made from apricot pits.

amatriciana: A traditional pasta sauce made with dried pork cheek

anatra: Duck

antipasto: A first course consisting of varieties of meats, cheeses, vegetables, and olives

aperitivo: An alcoholic beverage often consumed before meals and thought to stimulate the appetite and promote digestion

aragosta: Spiny lobster

arancine: Sicilian rice balls

arancio: Orange

arborio rice: An Italian short-grain rice that is synonymous with risotto.

arista: Roasted pork loin

arrabiata: A tomato based sauce made with chili peppers

arrosto: Roasted meat

asaigo: Mild cheese, often called the poor man's Parmigiano cheese

asparagi: Asparagus

B

baccalà: Salt cod

barbabietole: Beets

bagna cauda: A dipping sauce made with olive oil, butter, anchovies and garlic.

basilico: Basil

beciamella: Béchamel sauce. A white sauce made from butter and milk and thickened with flour.

Bel Paese: A creamy, light Italian cheese with a mild, sweet flavor

bierra: Beer

biscotti: Twice-baked cookies or biscuits

bistecca: Beef or veal steak seasoned with oil and pepper

bollito misto: A mixed boil of meat, chicken, veal, ham and tongue that are slowly simmered with carrots, onions, herbs and spices.

bolognese: A thick tomato based sauce with two or more different chopped meats such as beef, pork, veal, chicken livers and sausage simmered for hours with tomatoes, garlic, onions, mushrooms, wine and herbs.

braciola: Sliced beef, typically pan fried

branzino: Fish, usually sea bass, often cooked whole

brasato: Braised

bresaola: Cured raw beef similar in appearance to prosciutto. Most often it is served as an appetizer, sliced very thin and drizzled with lemon and olive oil.

brodetto: A rich soup or stew made with fish

brodo: Broth

bruschetta: Toasted garlic bread topped with chopped tomatoes, garlic, basil, and olive oil. It could also refer to any manner of toppings atop a toasted bread.

burro: Butter

c

cacciagione: Game

cacciatora: Meat, fish, or chicken cooked in a sauce that includes tomatoes, scallions,

mushrooms, and red or white wine

calzone: A baked or fried Italian turnover made from pizza dough and filled with meat, cheese, or vegetables

caffé espresso: Strong black coffee made by forcing hot steam through the ground coffee

caffé latte: Coffee and hot milk in equal parts

calamari: Squid

caldo: Warm or hot

cannella: Cinnamon

cannellini: White beans

cannelloni: Big tubes of pasta stuffed with a savory filling topped with a sauce and baked

cannoli: Tubes of crisp pastry filled with sweetened ricotta cheese, chocolate, or candied fruit

capelli d'angelo: Angel hair pasta

capitone: Large eel

caponata: A relish made of chopped eggplant, olives, onions, celery, and herbs in olive oil and served as an antipasto

capperi: Capers

cappuccino: Coffee and hot whipped milk

carbonara: A classic pasta sauce with bacon, eggs, cream, and grated cheese

carciofi: Artichokes

carmello: Burnt sugar

carne: Meat

carpaccio: Paper thin, raw beef

(alla) casalinga: Homemade

cassata alla siciliana: Rich Sicilian pound cake with layers of ricotta cheese

cassola: Seafood soup

castagna: Chestnut

cavolfiore: Cauliflower

cavolo: Often called cabbage but it looks more like kale

cedro: Citron

ceci: Garbonzo beans, chickpeas

cervella: Brains

cetriolo: Cucumber

chianti: A classic dry red wine

cicoria: Chicory

cinghiale: Wild boar

cioccolato: Chocolate

cipolla: Onion

cipollina: Pearl onion

concentrato purea di pomodoro: Tomato paste or tomato concentrate

coniglio: Rabbit

contorini: Vegetables accompanying the main course

coratella: Heart, lungs, liver, and kidney

coscetto: Leg; typically refers to lamb

costata: Rib chop

costoletta: Chop or cutlet

cotechino: Highly spiced pork sausage

cotto: Cooked, done

cozze: Mussels

crema: Cream or custard

crosta, crostata, or crostatina: Crust, pie crust

crostino: Small piece of toast

crostone: Large piece of toast

crudo: Raw

cucchiaio: Large spoon equaling a tablespoon

cucchiaino: Small spoon equaling a teaspoon

D

dolce: Sweet

dolci: Sweets, cakes

dragoncello: Tarragon

Dente, al: Well known Italian cooking term. It refers to the consistency of properly cooked pasta "to the tooth", tender but chewy.

E

eggplant rollatini: Eggplant stuffed with ricotta filling

erba: Herb

erba cipollina: Chives

espresso: Espresso is a process of extracting flavor from coffee beans. Served in very small cups, this is a dark, strong coffee made by forcing steam through finely ground, Italian-roast coffee.

estratto: Extract

F

fagioli: Dried kidney beans

fagiolini: String or French beans

farcito: Stuffed

farfalle: A dried pasta often called "bowtie" because of its shape

farina: Flour

fave: Broad beans

fegato: Liver

fegatini di polla: Chicken livers

ferri alla griglia: Grilled in cast iron pan

fettuccine: Broad, fresh long strand pasta commonly made from eggs and flour

fettuccine Alfredo: Fettuccine tossed with butter, heavy cream, and grated cheese

filetto: Fillet

finocchio: Fennel

focaccia: An Italian flatbread made by pressing a yeast-leavened dough onto a baking sheet, puncturing holes in it or dotting it and then lacing it with olive oil or any manner of herbs. It may also be topped with cheese, meat, or vegetables.

fontina: A firm textured cow's milk cheese with tiny holes and a slightly earthy flavor

formaggio: Cheese

fragola: Strawberry

freddo: Cold

fresco: Fresh, uncooked

friggere: To fry

fritata: Omelet

fritto: Fried

fritto misto: A mixture of small pieces of meat, seafood, and vegetables dipped in batter and fried

frittura: Fried food

frutta: Fruit

frutti di mare: an assortment of shellfish, the name means "fruit of the sea"

funghi: Mushrooms

fusilli: Spiral-shaped pasta

G

gamberi: Shrimp

gamberetti: Small shrimp

gelato: Italian ice cream

ghiaccio, ghiacciato: Ice; iced

gnocchi: Dumplings

Gorgonzola: One of the great Italian blue cheeses, blue-veined and either creamy or sharp

granchio: Crab

granita: Italian flavored ices

grappa: A clear liquor of high alcohol content, made by fermenting the grape skins after the juices have been drawn off

gremolata: An Italian garnish of minced parsley, lemon peel, and ground or chopped garlic

griglia: Grilled

grissini: Bread sticks

I

impanato: Breaded

imbottito: Stuffed

impastata ricotta: Known as the Cadillac of the ricottas. This fresh cheese is light as whipped cream and has the consistency and delicate flavor of soft sweet butter.

indivia: Endive

insalata: Salad

insalata di pomodoro: Salad with tomatoes

insalata mista: Mixed salad

involtini: Rolls of thinly sliced veal, pork, or fish cooked with a stuffing

L

lampone: Raspberries

lardo: Salt pork

lardo affumicato: Bacon

lasagna: A baked, layered pasta dish

latte: Milk

lattuga: Lettuce

lauro: Bay leaf

legumi: Vegetables

lenticchie: Lentils

lepre: Hare

lesso: Boiled meat

limoncello: An Italian citrus-based lemon liqueur that is served well chilled in the summer months. This is an absolutely natural product that is the result of the infusion of lemon skins in pure alcohol.

limone: Lemon

lobster tail: Italian bakeries in Little Italy in New York City created a pastry similar to the sfogliatelle, in the 1900's called a "lobster tail." The pastry has the same outside as a sfogliatelle, but instead of the ricotta filling, it is filled with a French cream similar to whipped cream.

lumache: Snails

M

maccheroni: Tube-shaped macaroni pasta

maggiorana: Marjoram

Marsala: A wine imported from Sicily and ranging from dry to sweet.

miale: Pork

maionese: Mayonnaise

mandorle: Almonds

manicotti: Large tube maccheroni stuffed with a ricotta cheese filling and baked

manzo: Beef

(alla) marinara: Sauce including tomato, garlic, oil and oregano

marinato: Marinated

mascarpone: A fresh, soft Italian cheese that is a delicately flavored triple cream cheese, rich, soft, and smooth in texture

mela: Apple

melanzana: Eggplant

melone: Melon

menta: Mint

merluzzo: Cod

miele: Honey

mille foglie: A flaky pastry, meaning "a thousand leaves"

minestra, minestre: The soup course of a meal

minestrone: Vegetable soup with pasta or rice

mirtillo: Blueberry

misto: Mixed

moleca: Soft shell crab

mortadella: Large, spiced pork sausage

mostaccioli: Two-inch pasta tubes with diagonally cut ends

mozzarella: A soft, delicately flavored white cheese

mozzarella di buffala: A version of mozzarella cheese, but made from buffalo milk

N

noce moscata: Nutmeg

nociole: Hazelnuts or filberts

Nutella®: A thick, smooth paste made from chocolate and hazelnuts

O

oca: Goose

olio: Oil

olio di olive: Olive oil. In Italy, olive oil is the most commonly used fat and is pressed from the pulp of ripe olives. Extra virgin olive oil is made by pressing the olives with no further processing. It is strictly regulated and produces oil with a very distinct flavor.

orecchiette: Pasta shaped like little ears, made from flour and water

origano: Oregano

orzo: Barley and pearl barley; also refers to small dried pasta, similar to rice but larger

osso bucco: Veal shanks braised with vegetables, aromatics, and stock. Osso bucco literally means "bone with a hole."

ostrica: Oysters

P

pancetta: Cured, spiced, but not smoked, this mild bacon is made from pork belly rolled into a tight cylindrical shape and cured for two months

pane: Bread

panforte: An Italian round, flat cake. filled with dried fruits, nuts, and spices. It contains a tiny amount of flour (just enough to hold the fruits and nuts together).

panettone: In Italian it means "big bread." A light-textured, spiced yeast bread containing raisins and candied fruit and served traditionally at Christmas and Easter.

panino: Bread roll

panna: Heavy cream

panna cotta: Italian pudding

panna montata: Whipped cream

pappardelle: Flat pasta cut into long ribbons

Parmigiano-Reggiano: Commonly called Parmesan cheese. One of the best known and most versatile of the hard cheeses.

pasta: Dough made of flour and water, which is used to make the many shapes of noodles

pasta all'uovo: Egg pasta

pasta asciutta: Dry pasta, served plain or with a little sauce

pasta in brodo: Pasta as part of a soup

pasta e fagioli: Soup with pasta and beans

pasticceria: Pastry shop

pasticcio: Baked dish with crust on top

pastina: Small pasta for soup

patata: Potato

pecorino: A salty, pleasant Italian sheep's milk cheese with a grainy texture usually grated or shaved

penne: Quill-shaped pasta

pepe nero: Black pepper

pepe rosso: Red pepper

peperoncini: Dried, hot peppers

peperone: Sweet peppers

pera: Pear

pesce: Fish

pesto: Paste made of fresh basil, garlic, olive oil, and Parmesan cheese

piccata: Thinly sliced veal or chicken with a lemon or Marsala sauce

pignoli: Pine nuts

pignoli cookies: Cookies made with almond paste and pine nuts; they do not contain flour

piselli: Baby peas

pistacchio: An edible pistachio nut from the evergreen pistacchio tree

pizza: A flat, yeasted bread that's baked with a variety of toppings, including tomato sauce, cheese, meats, vegetables, or seafood

pizzelle: Italian waffle cookies

(alla) pizzaiola: Meat or chicken cooked with tomato sauce, garlic, oregano, and black pepper

polenta: Italian cornmeal that is slow-cooked and can be served firm, fried, or as a soup.

polipi: Octopus

pollo: Chicken

polpette: Meatballs

polpettone: Meatloaf

pomodoro: Tomato

pompelmo: Grapefruit

porchetta: Whole roasted, boned and stuffed suckling pig

porcini: Italian mushrooms

portobello: A brown crimini

(courtesy of Order Sons of Italy in Amercia)

mushroom that is 4" - 6" in diameter

prezzemolo: Parsley

prosciutto: Cured ham

provolone: A mild Italian cheese, white in color, with a smooth texture

puttanesca: A piquant pasta sauce made of tomatoes, onions, black olives, capers, anchovies, and crushed red pepper flakes. The name puttanesca is a derivation of the word "puttana," which in Italian means "whore."

R

radicchio: Red chicory

ragu: Meat sauce

rana: Frog, often served fried or in risotto

rape: Turnips often roasted to bring out its sweetness

ravioli: Small squares (pillows) of pasta dough filled with meat, cheese, or vegetables to form little cushions and served with various sauces

ribollita: Tuscan bread soup

ricotta: Ricotta is a byproduct of cheese-making, and is made from reheating the leftover whey mixed with milk. It is creamy and smooth, and can be used in both sweet and savory dishes.

rigatoni: Larger than penne, but similar in shape, these are fat tubes of dried pasta with ridges

riso: Rice

risotto: Rice dish cooked by adding hot broth intermittently and stirring as the rice absorbs the liquid and becomes creamy. Usually made with saffron and served with grated cheese.

rosmarino: Rosemary

rotini: Corkscrew-shaped pasta

rotolo: A roll of meat or pasta, usually stuffed, and commonly poached

rucola: Arugula

S

salame: Salami

sale: Salt

salmone: Salmon

salsicce: Fresh sausage

saltare: Sauté

saltimbocca: A classic Italian way of cooking veal with prosciutto, sage, and wine. The name translates as "to jump in the mouth."

salvia: Sage

sambuca: A colorless Italian liqueur with a strong flavor of anise. Most often it's served with three coffee beans floating in the glass representing health, happiness, and prosperity.

sarde: Sardines

scaloppine: Thin slices of meat, especially veal

scampi: Prawns, a type of shrimp

scungilli: Edible part of a large gastropod mollusk or conch. The Italians refer to scungilli as whelk and the famous scungilli marinara is a garlicky dish of whelk cooked in a tomato sauce flavored with basil, oregano, and hot pepper seeds.

secco: Dry

sedano: Celery

sfogliatelle: Meaning many layers and resembling leaves, this flaky shell (mille foglie) is filled with a mixture of sweet ricotta cheese, eggs, sugar, and chopped citron

sformato: Sformato is derived from an Italian verb, sformare – "to unmold," yet its definition is elusive. The dish is baked in a mold (in a bain marie or double boiler), and has a texture between a soufflé and a flan, but it's not as airy and always contains beaten eggs. It can be a savory dish, with vegetables, pasta, potatoes, or rice, served as a side dish, or it can also be prepared as a sweet for dessert made with zabaglione, fruit, and chocolate, and served with a sauce.

semifreddo: Meaning 'half cold' and refers to any chilled or partially frozen desserts including cake, spumoni custard, whipped cream, or mousse

semolina: Yellow flour ground from durum wheat and used in making pasta

soffritto: A mixture of finely chopped onions, carrots, and celery sautéed in olive oil

sogliola: Sole

soppressata: Dry air-cured pork salami

spaghetti: Long, thin strands of dried or fresh pasta that is the most popular form of pasta

spaghettini: Very thin spaghetti

spezie: Spices

spiedino: To skewer and roast meat on a spit

spumante: Sparkling

spumone: Light ice cream often containing fruits and nuts

stracciatella: Roman egg drop soup

stracotto: Pot roast

strega: A bright yellow Italian liqueur with a bittersweet taste

strutto: Lard or butter, generally used for most Italian baking. Shortening is solid, white fat made from hydrogenated vegetable oil, and is more commonly found in North America.

stufato: Stew cooked on the stove

sugo: Gravy or sauce

T

tacchino: Turkey

tagliatelle: Long, flat, ribbon-like fresh pasta

tartufi: Truffles

testa: Head

timo: Thyme

tiramisu: A popular Italian dessert made with layers of mascarpone, zabaglione, lady fingers or sponge cake, and moistened with strong espresso-rum syrup. In Italian, tiramisu means "pick me up."

tonno: Tuna fish

torrone: Nougat made from honey, whipped egg whites, vanilla, and walnuts or almonds

torta: Cake or tart

tortellini: Small stuffed pasta nuggets filled with various ingredients, usually meat or cheese

trippa: Tripe

trota: Trout

truffle: A delicacy grown underground in parts of Italy and used sparingly as a garnish

U

uovo: Egg

uva: grapes

uva passa: Raisins

V

vaniglia: Vanilla, used almost exclusively as a flavoring for pastries and desserts in Italy, both from a bottled extract or preferably, utilizing the scraped seeds from fresh vanilla beans

verdura: Usually refers to green, leafy vegetables, as well as garden produce in general, including legumes and roots

vermicelli: Literally translated as "little worms," it is the name for very thin spaghetti, less than a tenth of an inch thick

vino: Wine

vitello: Milk-fed young veal

vitello tonato: Chilled veal in a tuna and anchovy sauce

vongole: Clams

W

whelk: A large marine gastropod that Italians commonly refer to as scungilli

Z

zabaglione: A frothy Italian dessert of egg yolks, sugar, and Marsala wine

zafferano: Saffron

zeppole: A Neapolitan fritter

ziti: Tubular maccheroni originally from Southern Italy

zucchero: Sugar

zucchini: A long, green squash that looks something like a cucumber

zuppa Inglese: A desert made of custard and cake, a variation on the British dessert known as trifle. The phrase "zuppa Inglese" literally means "English soup."

ACKNOWLEDGMENTS

Grazie tanto

My love for all things Italian began in 1962 when I spent one month in Italy. That's all it took for me to become a passionate Italianophile. I chose Italian as my language requirement in college and thus began my love affair with a fabulous country and its people. I admire and appreciate the language, the music, the art, the love of life and of family and, of course, the food. I am not Italian, so I hope the readers will be gentle if I falter in the nuance of their culture, but I do love history and food and I love to cook, and eat, and write, and research. The book took me on a journey and served to remind me of the joy I experienced while living in Italy.

America's Little Italys was an exhilarating and rewarding endeavor. There are many, many people to thank from the restaurant and shop owners — who sat with me and told the story of their family, their business and provided photography and shared recipes — to the manufacturers and organizations who supplied information and logos. If anyone has been excluded or if any restaurant, shop, or bakery has been left out, I apologize. For those that shared their stories with me thank you so very much!

From the very beginning, my daughter Lauren Juceam was there for me and for this book as she slipped into her role as my advisor, therapist, personal editor, and recipe tester. I am also indebted to Gary Goldenstein, for his patience and calm help with my computer. And big thanks to Joel, Allison, Brian, Debbie, Daniel, Sammy, Harry, Joshua and Andy for just being my family, and to the staff at Seller's Publishing for thinking that this book was worthy of their interest.

My gratitude goes to: Connie Artuso, Francis Roselli, Lou and Sal DiPalo, Giovanna DiBona, Chris Gomez, Sal Esposito, Robert Ianniello, Peter Lepore, Vincent Generoso, Tina Aprea, Bob Alleva, Buddy Greco, John and Mike Brescio, Greg and Ben Garofolo, Sonny Bari, Frank Castallana, Danny Moceri, Mario Cefalu, Joe Bucillacci, Nancy Nichols, Daniella Levenson, Dominick Brunetto, Andrea Wakefield, Lois Ellis, Carol Gaeta, Alan Constantino, Lisa Morekas, Chef Leonardo Kern, Pat Coffey, Christopher Borgatti, Mario Borgatti, Gil and Michael Teitel, Carmela Lucciola, Sal Florio Jr., Joseph Miglucci, David Greco, Nancy Phillips, David Ruccio, Sarah Wiggen, Pat DeSteffano, Connie LaRussa, Ed Dispigno, Bill Mignucci Jr., Joan Aiazzi, Charles Gitto Jr., Tony and Sande Nitti, Chef Gianni Audieri, Bob Larive, Fabio Giotta, Michael Di Camillo, Wendy Chataline, Barbara Consiglio, Charlotte Piazza, Filippo Berio®, Nutella®, Calabro Cheese®, La Bella San Marzano®, Lazzaroni®, BelGioioso Cheese, A.G.Ferrari Foods, IllyUSA®, Chef Boyardee®, San Pellegrino®, Acqua Panna®, ColavitaUSA®, GrupoCampari®, Del Grosso Foods®, DeCecco®, Torani®, Lavazza®, Prince®, Progresso®, Order Sons of Italy in America, Missouri Historical Society and Jason Stratman, Dr. Joseph V. Scelsa and the Italian American Museum, Joseph Muratore and the Rhode Island Historical Society, Sal Serio and the New Orleans American Italian Museum and Research Library, San Diego Little Italy Association, Major General Francis A. Ianni and Catherine Tripalin Murray.